BEST
TEA SHOP WALKS
IN DORSET

Norman & June Buckley

Published by Sigma Leisure – an imprint of
Sigma Press, 1 South Oak Lane, Wilmslow, Cheshire SK9 6AR, England.

British Library Cataloguing in Publication Data
A CIP record for this book is available from the British Library.

ISBN: 1-85058-648-9

Typesetting and Design by: Sigma Press, Wilmslow, Cheshire.

Cover: street scene, Abbotsbury.

Maps: Alan Bradley

Photographs: the authors

Printed by: MFP Design and Print

Disclaimer: the information in this book is given in good faith and is believed to be correct at the time of publication. No responsibility is accepted by either the author or publisher for errors or omissions, or for any loss or injury howsoever caused. Only you can judge your own fitness, competence and experience.

Preface

In adding books to this popular county-by-county series, it is obviously that some areas have a higher suitability and, therefore, priority than others. To the authors it seemed inevitable that the home of the celebrated Dorset Cream Tea was a prime target for early inclusion. In every way as much 'tea shop country' as the adjacent Devon (already covered in two volumes), the possibly slightly underestimated county of Dorset has proved to be an excellent choice in every respect.

Of course, good tea shop country has to be accompanied by at least equally good walking country. In this regard Dorset has not been found wanting. The South West Coast Path threads its way beautifully along the striking coastline, which includes the highest sea cliff on the south coast of England, giving a basis for a series of fine circular walks. Inland, the extensive Wessex downland and the lovely villages provide more than enough to satisfy walking appetites and, hopefully, to stimulate tea shop appetites at the same time.

The 28 routes in the book, ranging in length from 1½ to 9 miles do, therefore, offer the diversity which is part and parcel of walking at the easier end of the scale, from a stroll in the grounds of a stately home to more demanding downland circuits. All are circular and many do offer shorter or longer variations; none include rough scrambling and all should be well within the capability of the average rambler.

Having said that, I must repeat my usual advice about walking in proper boots with good soles. Those with lightweight canvas uppers should be ideal for Dorset, at least in summer. It may have something to do with my Lake District mountain background, but I do always carry a compass. Surprisingly, on occasion this is useful in Dorset, where there are many prairie-like fields and a simple compass bearing can help in heading accurately for the next objective. Whilst the sketch maps and the text are sufficient to follow the described routes, the use of an Ordnance Survey map does enhance the understanding and enjoyment of the surrounding countryside.

On the subject of farmers' fields, despite the efforts of the local authority and of local ramblers' groups, every country walker will,

from time to time, encounter situations where a right of way footpath has disappeared, either under the plough or the ensuing crop.
Field edges may also be ploughed tight to the boundary. Dorset is
probably no better or worse than other areas in this regard, but it is
particularly annoying to find designated footpaths such as the Ramblers' Association 'Jubilee Trail' badly affected in places.

I must admit that I do sometimes wonder about the proliferation
of designated footpaths; some, such as the Pennine Way, and in this
book, the South West Coast Path, are entirely logical and offer mar-
vellous continuity over a long distance, with a true sense of purpose.
Others encountered in Dorset include the Jubilee Trail, the Monarch's Way, the Hardy Trail, the Brit Valley Circular Walk, the Liberty Way and the Wessex Ridgeway. With the possible exception of
the last of these routes, these seem to be questionable concepts, particularly as some sections are not well maintained and appear to be
little used. Waymarking in the county is generally good.

To match the variety of the walks, the same consideration has
been applied to tea shops. Whilst everyone enjoys the rich ambi-
ence of a good traditional English tea shop, which inevitably form
the majority, this book, like others in the series, is at pains to intro-
duce walkers to premises such as craft centres, a renovated corn
mill, a farm, a stately home, a tank museum and a field studies centre. What a tempting array!

Likewise, with regard to the actual refreshments, the Dorset
cream tea is fundamental; indistinguishable from the Devon variety,
rich clotted cream is, of course essential to accompany the
home-made scones and strawberry jam. However, the modern de-
mand for a variety of catering throughout the day, preferably including some savoury items, must be acknowledged and the assessment
of the recommended tea shops comments accordingly.

The layout of the book includes a quick check section at the start
of each walk. This summarises these various characteristics in such
a way that an informed choice of walk and tea shop can rapidly be
made. The following 'About the area' gives a concise description of
the towns or villages on or close to the route of the walk and of any
notable landscape features or visitor attractions.

The other essential advice is to recommend a parking place for
motor vehicles, however much one might wish to favour the use of
public transport. The selection is made with care and with a grid reference for positive location.

Concerning public transport, there are two railway lines through the county that could be of use to walkers. One is the London (Waterloo) to Bournemouth and Weymouth line, with stations at Wareham, Wool, Moreton, Dorchester, Upwey and Weymouth. Of these, Wareham, Moreton and Upwey are all reasonably close to walks (nos. 20, 21, 11, respectively) in this book. Services are quite frequent, generally at regular intervals. The other line leaves the Western main line at Castle Cary to run via Yeovil and Dorchester to Weymouth. Other than Upwey, no stations relate directly to the walks; services are normally from Bristol to Weymouth, where there are good bus connections to the Isle of Portland. All Tourist Information Centres have information about bus services.

Norman & June Buckley

Contents

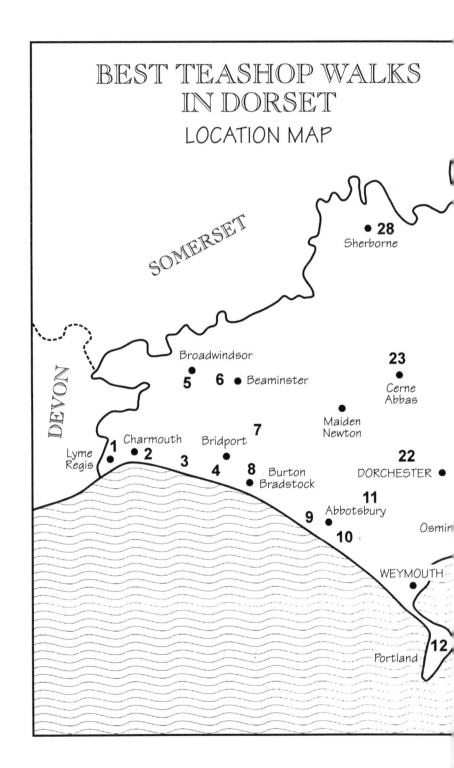

BEST TEASHOP WALKS
IN DORSET
LOCATION MAP

SOMERSET

DEVON

● **28**
Sherborne

Broadwindsor
●
5   **6** ● Beaminster

23
●
Cerne
Abbas

●
Maiden
Newton

7

Lyme   **1**   Charmouth   Bridport
Regis   ● **2**   ●
              3   **4**   **8** ● Burton
                              ● Bradstock

22
DORCHESTER ●

11
●
Abbotsbury
9 ●
    10   Osmir

WEYMOUTH
●

12

Portland

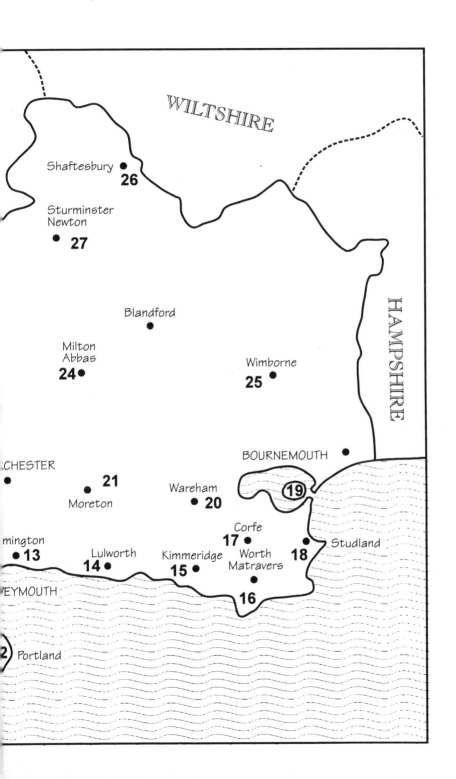

WILTSHIRE

Shaftesbury ●
26

Sturminster
Newton
● **27**

Blandford
●

Milton
Abbas
24●

Wimborne
25 ●

HAMPSHIRE

BOURNEMOUTH ●

.CHESTER
●

21
●

Wareham
● **20**

19

Corfe
17 ●

Moreton

Worth
Matravers

18 ●

Studland

mington
● **13**

Lulworth
14 ●

Kimmeridge
15 ●

16

.EYMOUTH

2 Portland

Introduction

It is probably true to say that Dorset is one of England's lesser-known holiday counties. Apart from the huge area of Bournemouth, Poole and Christchurch, which is hardly characteristic of the county as a whole, Dorset is quiet and discreet, yielding its charms only to those who seek them out. Without motorway and with minimal railway services, Dorset is never likely to rival Devon or Cornwall as a West Country holiday destination. But what delights there are for those whose interests coincide with the purpose of this book!

Landscape

The landscape is defined by great ridges of limestone, most notably the South Wessex Downs, running roughly from north-east to south-west across the county. Never reaching 300m, and often closer to 200m in height, this broad upland has a profound effect on the farming of the middle part of the county. To the north is the richer lowland, such as the Vale of Marshwood, fringed by hills such as Pilsdon Pen and Lewesdon, whilst to the south there are extensive areas of characteristic heathland. Close to the coast, another ridge of chalk/limestone forms the long, narrow, line of the Purbeck Hills, extending from the fine cliffs of the Foreland, between Swanage and Studland, to Worbarrow Bay, where it converges with another ridge which actually forms the Purbeck coastline.

The Dorset coastline extends for about 70 miles, much of which is of such high scenic value that an official 'Heritage Coast' designation has been applied. In the east is the huge expanse of Poole Harbour, studded with islands such as Brownsea and the playground for flotillas of sailing boats. At the western extremity is Lyme Regis and its bay, fringed by great, unstable, fossil-rich cliffs. In between is constant delight, the perfect gem of Lulworth Cove, the bleak St Aldhelm's Head, Chesil Bank with the ancient swannery at Abbotsbury and, highest of all, the glowing Golden Cap. Extending for four miles into the English Channel, the great lump of solid limestone which is the Isle of Portland has a history and character all of its own.

The county is not noted for important rivers; best known is the River Stour, which rises in neighbouring Wiltshire before passing Sturminster Newton, wriggling past the downland close to Blandford Forum and reaching the sea at Christchurch.

Human Occupation

To the observant visitor it is very obvious that Dorset is an 'old' county, with evidence of human activity well back into the mists of pre-history. A visit to Maiden Castle or a view of the Cerne Abbas giant are just two of the most popular manifestations. The Stone Age has left monuments such as Eggardon and two long barrows at Hambledon Hill, reminding us of the proximity to Wiltshire, arguably the cradle of pre-historic human activity in Britain. Remains of the ensuing Bronze Age are prolific; for example, many barrows of around 1500BC are concentrated along the ridge which is marked by the Hardy monument. Even more striking and a great Dorset landscape feature are the Iron Age hill forts, in such number and concentration to suggest comparatively dense occupation of the area during the 1000 years or so up to the Roman conquest. Pilsdon Pen, Badbury Rings and Poundbury are good examples, but finest of all is Maiden Castle near Dorchester, known to have been attacked and captured by the Romans under Vespasian in AD 43/44. During the Roman occupation of the county, they established the towns of Dorchester (Durnovaria) and Wareham, with the four main streets in the pattern of a cross in each case.

Like most coastal counties, Dorset had its share of Saxon and Danish invaders, using Poole Harbour as a convenient access. The earth ramparts still evident at Wareham were vital in defending the town, as the Rivers Frome and Piddle (Trent) allowed raiders to approach from Poole Harbour. This was the time of King Alfred, a Wessex man, recorded by the Anglo-Saxon Chronicle as pursuing Danish raiding forces across Dorset towards Exeter.

In medieval times Dorset had relatively few great castles; notable were Sherborne and Corfe, the latter being owned by King John and used for some of his worst atrocities. Abbeys were quite widely established, well known examples being at Sherborne, Shaftesbury, Cerne Abbas, Milton and Abbotsbury. Whilst these Abbeys no doubt exerted considerable secular power and, in some cases owned large estates, there is little evidence of the widespread dominance wielded by some of the great northern Abbeys such as Fountains or Furness. Remains can be seen in all these places.

Sir Walter Raleigh was probably Dorset's best known resident in Elizabethan times. Sherborne Castle was his home; before his unfortunate execution he commenced the construction of the 'new' castle there.

In the 1640s, the Civil War raged throughout Dorset, with numerous small skirmishes between predominantly local people supporting the opposing sides, rather than the great pitched battles which determined the eventual outcome of the war. Well documented are the wanderings of King Charles II throughout the county, after his defeat at the Battle of Worcester, avoiding capture as he attempted to escape to France. In Charles's case the escape was made and the eventual outcome of the Restoration of the Monarchy was happy for him. It was not so for his unfortunate son the Duke of Monmouth. His landing at Lyme Regis in 1685 and his attempt to regain the Crown for the Stuarts led to defeat at the Battle of Sedgemoor, capture in Dorset and death on Tower Hill.

In more recent times the list of notable residents is headed by Thomas Hardy, novelist supreme, who spent most of his life in and around Dorchester, capturing the rhythm and pace of rustic Dorset life to perfection and using his deep knowledge of the local towns and villages to create background authenticity. The names were changed but most are recognisable and well documented.

Another Dorset resident with enduring fame was the enigmatic scholar/soldier/writer T.E. Lawrence (of Arabia), whose World War I exploits in the desert are the very stuff of schoolboy heroics. Less well known but nevertheless honoured by a great monument, was Sir Thomas Masterman Hardy, Nelson's flag captain at the Battle of Trafalgar and resident of a nearby village.

Few can remember individual names but, collectively, the Tolpuddle Martyrs are known throughout the land. Sentenced to seven years transportation in 1834, six agricultural labourers later achieved nation-wide fame and became a foundation stone of the emerging trade union movement. Their alleged offence was to administer an oath which was illegal under the Mutiny Act of 1797, but the real worry of local employers and magistrates was that the men had been instrumental in forming a trade union, the Friendly Society of Agricultural Labourers, with the objective of resisting further reductions in agricultural wages, which had fallen drastically during the previous four years. As trade unions had, in themselves, been legal since 1824, the oath charge was merely a device for getting rid of these inconvenient men for as long a period as possible. In the event, the public outcry was such that within two years full pardons had been granted and the men eventually returned to Dorset. There is a Martyrs' Museum and TUC Memorial Cottages on the main street in Tolpuddle village.

The Thomas Hardy memorial, Higher Bockhampton

1. Lyme Regis and Uplyme

Length	6½ miles
Summary	A walk for those who enjoy a ramble through peaceful countryside, away from the hurly-burly of the nearby holiday coast. Lanes, good paths and the odd minor road combine to make an attractive route through the Lyme Regis hinterland, including Uplyme village. There are no serious ascents, although a height of 185m (607ft.) is reached and there are several minor ups and downs.
Car Parking	Large pay and display car park with public conveniences at the western end of Lyme Regis, entered from the main road, just beyond the junction with the road leading down to the Cobb. Grid reference, 337920.
Maps	Ordnance Survey Explorer no. 29, Lyme Regis and Bridport, 1:25,000 or Landranger no. 193, Taunton and Lyme Regis, 1:50,000.

Tea Shop

As expected, the popular seaside resort of Lyme Regis has many cafés and it was quite difficult to select just one. Bell Cliff Tea Shop enjoys a unique situation – a kind of island building at the lower end of the main street, perched above the promenade. It is a simply furnished tea room – plain wood furniture and pleasing crockery. The speciality of the Bell Cliff is the enormous portion of Dorset apple cake, reputedly the best in the county, always served hot and with clotted cream. The Victorian afternoon tea includes cucumber or tomato sandwiches, coffee or chocolate sponge cake and a pot of tea; alternatively one can opt for the usual cream tea, toasted teacakes, or choose from a selection of cakes. Cooked meals such as ham, egg and chips or corned beef hash may appeal depending on the weather and time of day.

Open: 9.00am – 5.30pm every day from Easter to end of October but closes earlier on winter afternoons. Tel. 01297 442459

Bell Cliff Tea Shop

About the Area

Lyme Regis has long been a favourite resort, beautifully situated on Lyme Bay in a hollow between great, unstable, wooded cliffs. The town has a long history, appearing in records of Sherborne Abbey well before the Norman Conquest and being made a free borough by King Edward I in 1284, with the prestigious addition of 'Regis' to its name.

Perhaps the most distinctive historic feature is the 'Cobb', the massive sheltering breakwater enclosing a snug little harbour which, in one form or another has been here for well over 600 years. The present structure dates largely from the 19th century, being substantially renewed after a storm had caused great damage.

Despite long interludes as little more than a sleepy fishing village, overall Lyme has had more than its share of incident. During the Civil War West Dorset was a place of battles and skirmishes as both sides had significant local support and then, in 1685, the Duke of Monmouth landed here in his doomed attempt to seize the crown.

As the 18th century progressed, the town became a fashionable watering place, attracting among its visitors Jane Austin who featured it in her novel 'Persuasion'. More recently, the popular film 'The French Lieutenant's Woman', with the dramatic sequence of Meryl Streep on the Cobb, has revived literary interest in this most photogenic of places.

More enduring is the well-earned reputation as Britain's greatest fossil hunting centre. Mary Anning was by no means the first successful hunter in the area, but her discovery of the amazing ichthyosaurus in 1811, when she was just 10 years old, caught the public imagination and put the town into the spotlight yet again. Ever since this find people with little hammers may be seen chipping away on the beach and adjacent cliffs.

The present town is a jumble of houses and little streets, many of them old, climbing the hillside, and most attractively seen from the Cobb or the adjacent sandy beach. The variety of colours of the walls of the houses facing the sea gives an almost Mediterranean appearance. Fortunately, little has changed in recent years and commercial 'amusements' are minimal. Traditional features such as sea fishing, a marine aquarium and a local history museum with a good fossil collection add to rather than detract from Lyme as a destination for visitors.

Uplyme is a quiet residential village about two miles inland and the surrounding countryside, with farms and the odd former water-powered mill, is attractive.

The Walk

Cross the main road and follow Pound Road as far as another main road. Cross and go into Wadmead Road opposite. In 30m turn left through a kissing gate and take a well defined footpath descending over grass. Reach a surfaced road and turn right. Cross the River Lim and turn left along a minor surfaced road by the river. There are 'Liberty Trail' and 'Wessex Ridgeway' waymarks. There is a waymarked permissive path beside this road.

Go straight ahead at a junction of paths. After bollards the route continues along a footpath. Go over two footbridges to a gate/stile and cross a meadow. Haye Farm is above to the left. After another signposted kissing gate and a footbridge over the river, fork left by a former water-powered mill to go up to a gate/stile and continue along a footpath, now apparently part of the 'East Devon Way'! It has to be admitted that in a Dorset book this crossing of the county boundary is an undoubted transgression requiring an apology to the author of the South Devon book in this series. The apology having been accepted, we are now free to continue.

Go through woodland to reach the outskirts of Uplyme on Mill Lane. Go straight across a road to a path signposted 'to the church'. At the next public road turn right, uphill, to walk to the church. By the church go left, downhill, passing the school. As the road bends sharp left at Cooks Mead, go right, into a lane with a cul de sac sign. Keep right at a fork in a few metres, heading for Carswell Farm.

The lane provides good walking, rising gently above Carswell Bottom and Roccombe Bottom, which seem to be alternative names for the same valley. Go through the farm and rise more steeply as the lane gradually loses its surface. About half a mile after the farm go through two gates in quick succession. Immediately after the second gate turn right through a little gate and follow a minor path downhill past bluebells and butterflies to a wider gate. Pass several houses and ascend a surfaced driveway to join a public road.

In 10m fork left up to a gate with a 'public footpath' signpost to follow a little path through bramble; there are views to Uplyme. On approaching woodland bend left to an obvious signpost and gate. Cross a minor road to a broad track opposite – the 'Coach Road'. Continue to a 'T' junction and turn right to descend to Harcombe Road.

Turn left then, in 20m, turn right at a 'public footpath' signpost to go down the access drive to Lower Rhode Farm. Go to the farm and turn right through a kissing gate with signpost. Follow ' Rhode Barton and Lyme Regis', straight on over a stile and across a meadow, veering a little to the right to another signpost, stile and a footbridge over a tree-flanked stream in the bottom.

Exit past a waymarked post and follow the path up the field ahead to Rhode Barton, reached through a waymarked gate, cattle-churned ground and a waymarked gate/stile. Join the 'Liberty Trail/Wessex Ridgeway' and turn right to go between buildings on an unsurfaced lane. Continue along an avenue of sycamore and horse chestnut

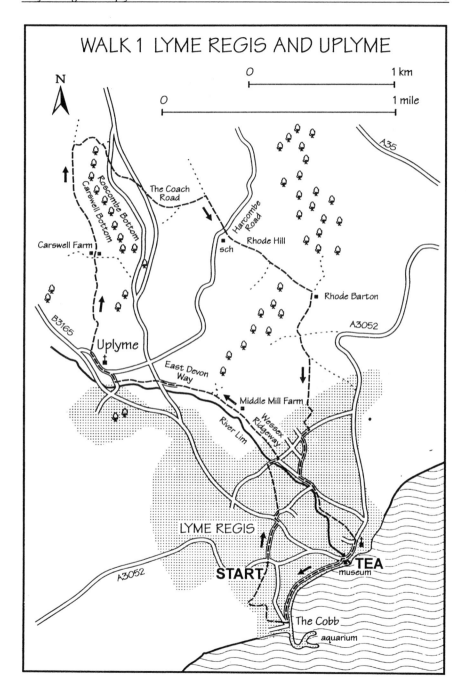

WALK 1 LYME REGIS AND UPLYME

trees. Go straight across a cross paths and, in 200m, turn right at a kissing gate with 'public footpath' signpost to take a path descending across a large meadow to a residential area.

Go through a gate at the bottom corner and turn right, downhill, along a residential road. Turn left at the first junction into Colway Close and continue along a pedestrian way at the end of the Close. Carry on down to another road. Turn right, still descending, and then left into North Avenue. At the bottom turn left and then right at the first road junction into Woodmead Road.

Turn left in 20m along the side of the River Lim. Cross a footbridge and go along a lovely little old street – Mill Green. Pass the Angel Inn and go ahead to 'Riverside Walk Town Mill' along a causeway between the river and a mill leat. On the right is the Leper Well. Reach the former town mill, now used for other purposes, follow the roadway to Combe Street and turn right to reach the main street by the traffic lights.

Turn right to the tea shop, which is in a prominent position.

To return to the car park the shortest and easiest route is straight up the main street. The more attractive route is along the sea front to the harbour and then either up the road or through the Cobb car park, past the bowling green. Turn right up the steps, with 'coast path' signposts, then up more steps by the side of a tumbling stream. At a waymarked stile bear right, then right again to go through a gate and along a residential road straight to the car park.

---

2. Charmouth and Chardown Hill

Length   4 ¼ miles

Summary   A walk including a fine part of the South West Coast Path, with spectacular evidence of landslips, the inland Chardown Hill, and the National Trust area of Stonebarrow Hill, with its shop and information centre. Not a very long walk but with some quite demanding ascents to heights of 140m (459ft.) and 190m (624ft) from near sea level. Apart from some cattle-churned ground, this route is first class underfoot throughout, with a short length of roadside walking in Charmouth village.

Car Parking   Reasonably priced large pay and display car park with public conveniences in Lower Sea Lane, Charmouth, grid reference 365935. Alternative car park behind beach at end of Lower Sea Lane- rather more expensive.

Maps   Ordnance Survey Explorer no. 29, Lyme Regis and Bridport, 1:25,000 or Landranger no. 193, Taunton and Lyme Regis, 1:50,000.

Tea Shop

Stow House, a 17th century building, is towards the bottom of the main street in Charmouth. The tea room is traditional and pleasant but on sunny days the tranquil rear garden is the place to be. Maureen and Derrick Kent have been the proprietors for twelve years and appear to enjoy their work and find time to chat to customers whilst giving efficient service. At lunch time the menu includes soup, sandwiches, salad with a choice of ham, tuna, or pizza. The afternoon menu offers sandwiches, cream teas, home-made cakes, buttered toast. Beverages offered are cafétière, instant, or decaffeinated coffee, choice of teas, hot chocolate, and cold drinks. Walkers are welcome but are requested, quite understandably, not to walk through the house wearing muddy boots.

Open: Easter weekend then from the end of May to end of September 10.30am to 5pm every day but always closed on Wednesday. Also open early and late season but days and hours are variable. Closed all winter months. Tel. 01297 560603.

About the Area

Strung for some distance along a rising section of the former A35, the substantial village and resort of Charmouth has been greatly improved by the construction of a by-pass a few years ago.

Although less well-known than its near neighbour Lyme Regis, from which it is separated by the unstable cliffs of the Spittles and Black Venn, the village does have some historic claims and there are many attractive cottages and larger Georgian/Regency houses. The Queens Armes Inn is of Tudor origin, allegedly giving hospitality to Catherine of Aragon in 1501 and to the future King Charles II in 1651 when he was waiting for a ship in which to escape to France.

Charmouth shares with Lyme the distinction of being the fossil hunting 'capital' of Britain; Mary Anning's ichthyosaurus was discovered in the blue lias cliffs of Black Venn. A museum in the village has a good array of local fossil specimens. With its unspoilt sandy beaches, Charmouth is also popular as a family resort – 'sweet and retired' according to Jane Austin.

Morcombelake, reached by an extension to this walk, is a village on high ground between Charmouth and Chideock. It is noted for Moore's biscuit factory, which produces 'Dorset Knobs' and other local delicacies. The factory has become a popular visitor attraction.

The tea shop at Charmouth

The Walk

Turn right out of the car park to head towards the sea. Turn left immediately before the beach car park along a surfaced footpath with a 'Coast path. Golden Cap 3' signpost. This path is also part of the 'Monarch's Way'. Cross the River Char on a footbridge to take a narrow path rising ahead, with a 'Seaton 4' signpost.

The climb to Cain's Folly, brightened by bluebells and cowslips, is entirely clear on the ground. From above, the landslipped area, so typical of this part of the Dorset coast, is very impressive. There are good views back over Charmouth and, as the top is reached, the Isle of Portland comes into view. For obvious reasons keep well back from this and, indeed, all cliff edges in Dorset.

At a signpost keep straight on towards 'Golden Cap 2', soon descending quite steeply, including a few steps. For a short distance the path becomes rather vague; keep close to the cliff, cross a small footbridge, then a second bridge, before rising again. Cross a stream on yet another bridge and ascend a slope.

At the top turn left, just before a stile, to follow a 'Stone Barrow Hill and Morcombelake' signpost. Go over grass initially and then up a gently rising lane to a gate to continue the ascent on a broad, cattle-churned path, heading for a hill. At a signposted gate, join an unsurfaced lane.

If a shorter walk avoiding Chardown Hill appeals, turn left along this lane to go directly to Stone Barrow Hill.

To continue, turn right at the lane, then quickly left to follow a steep uphill track signposted 'bridle way to Morcombelake'. At the top bear left around the rim of Chardown Hill on a well worn track.

If a visit to Morcombelake is desired, go through two gates in quick succession on the right, where a signpost points the way along the side of a fence. The main A35 road and the biscuit factory are about one third of a mile distant.

The basic route continues over chalky ground towards Stone Barrow Hill and, beyond, Charmouth, through swathes of bluebells, with bramble and gorse. Go through a farm gate and on through a waymarked gate, over well-cropped grass. Through another gate is a major junction of tracks and the limit of vehicular access through the National Trust Stone Barrow area. There is a 'Charmouth 1¼' signpost.

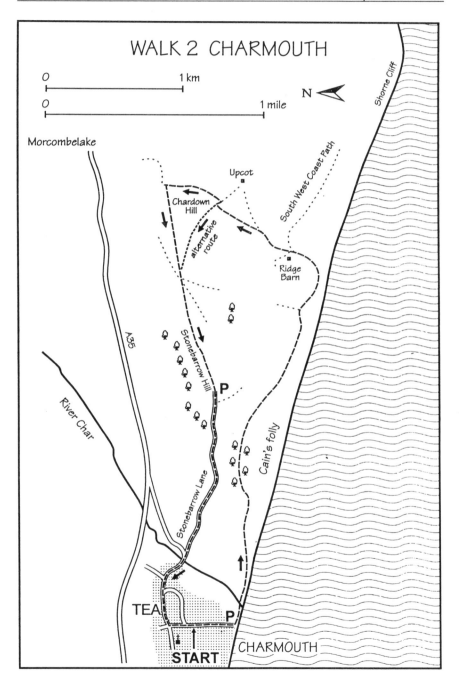

WALK 2 CHARMOUTH

0 ⊢————————————⊣ 1 km

0 ⊢————————————————⊣ 1 mile

N

Shorne Cliff

Morcombelake

Upcot

Chardown Hill

alternative route

South West Coast Path

Ridge Barn

A35

Stonebarrow Hill

P

River Char

Cain's folly

Stonebarrow Lane

TEA

P

START

CHARMOUTH

Carry straight on along the unsurfaced lane, passing the main car parking areas and the National Trust information centre/shop, open at Easter and from May to October. Stay with Stone Barrow Lane, which soon becomes surfaced, and descend, quite steeply in places, towards Charmouth. In Spring the verges are alive with wild flowers. Reach the Charmouth main village street at the bottom and turn left. Cross the River Char and rise for a short distance to find the tea shop on the right.

After refreshment continue uphill to the junction with Lower Sea Lane; turn left to return to whichever car park has been chosen.

3. Seatown and Golden Cap

Length	3½ miles
Summary	Those who enjoy coastal walking in Dorset (there can't be many walkers who don't!) really do have to climb Golden Cap, because it's there, if for no better reason. This short walk combines this magnificent section of coast with the woodland of Langdon Hill and the coastal hamlet of Seatown. Excellent tracks throughout.
Car Parking	Free National Trust car park in the woodland of Langdon Hill, grid reference 412930. Accessed from A35 by an unsignposted minor road between Chideock and Morcambelake. Alternatively, if time on the beach is to be combined with the walk, there is a pay car park at Seatown, grid reference 421918.
Maps	Ordnance Survey Explorer no. 29, Lyme Regis and Bridport, 1:25,000 or Landranger no. 193, Taunton and Lyme Regis, 1:50,000.

Tea Shops

Having accepted that Golden Cap was a "must", finding a tea shop proved to be a problem so refreshment arrangements are something of a compromise. If wanting food and drink part way round the walk call at The Anchor Inn at Seatown – typical pub grub here and nothing wrong with that – everything from crisps, sandwiches, to full cooked meals not forgetting tea, coffee, and ices. This is a relatively small inn with masses of outdoor seating – a popular hostelry. Open: food available from 12noon to 9.30pm every day from end of May to early September; remainder of the year 12noon – 2pm and evenings.

The alternative is to complete the walk and then drive down to Batchworth House in Chideock. Travelling downhill towards Bridport the car park for Batchworth House is on the right of the road – just look for the "cream tea" signs. Park, and then walk across the main road and up the hill for twenty five metres to find Batchworth House. Just ring the bell of this lovely seventeenth century building to receive a warm welcome from hosts Ann and Bob Harvey. There is a well furnished dining room but through the house is a sheltered tea garden and this is first choice on sunny afternoons. Dorset cream teas are offered or one might prefer toasted teacakes served with butter and jam or home made cakes.

Open: 2.30pm – 5.30pm every day from Easter to end of October and weekends only during the other months. Tel. 01297 489478.

About the Area

Golden Cap, at 191m (627ft.) the south coast's highest hill, is the crowning glory of the Dorset coastline. Not only its height, but its dominant position, its shape and its wonderful colouring all contribute to the distinction. It links well with the contrasting Langdon Hill just a short distance inland, long, wooded and self-effacing. This hill is a National Trust enterprise, planted largely with Corsican Pine and beech in the 1960s. The rich botany includes several kinds or orchid.

Seatown is just a tiny fishing hamlet but with the wide ranging facilities of the popular Anchor Inn.

Chideock is off the strict line of this walk, although some walkers

The Anchor Inn, Seatown

will no doubt divert to visit the village as suggested under 'Tea Shops', above. It is a pleasant village, beautifully situated and with thatched cottages and other attractive buildings. The former Chideock Castle is now just a grassy mound following its capture and destruction by Parliamentary forces in 1645. A small 19th century Roman Catholic church has an interesting mortuary chapel and striking interior decoration.

As the village main street is the A35, local people are understandably campaigning hard for a by-pass.

The Walk

Leave the car park at the top left-hand corner by the information boards, by a broad level forest track signposted 'coast path. Golden cap ¾.' The views include Ridge Cliff and Doghouse Hill, east of Seatown. As the track rises gently through woodland carpeted with bluebells in May, Golden Cap comes into view.

As the track bends right, by a seat, go down to the left to a signpost 'to coast path and Golden Cap' Follow a little path to join a more major track in a few metres. Turn right and go through a gate to take the obvious path up Golden Cap. There is a gate and a signpost before the summit is reached; the last lap is assisted by steps.

Make for the trig. point and the 'Seatown 1' marker stone. One hundred and fifty metres to the west (right) is a plaque dedicated to the Earl of Antrim, chairman of the National Trust from 1966-77, in whose memory Golden Cap was given to the Trust. On a clear day the views are superb, including the Isle of Portland and, much further, Start Point in Devon. Inland, Pilsdon Pen, with its Iron Age fort, is visible.

Descend the same length of path, with the steps, to the signpost. Turn right for 'Seatown 1' and take a narrow path over grass. The way is very obvious, first over a double stile and then a grass track with the occasional stile and signpost. Towards the bottom there has been a diversion of the old path; follow the waymarks through a little woodland and across a field to reach the Seatown access road. Turn right to reach the Anchor Inn (and the Seatown car park) in a short distance.

From the Inn walk back up the access road for about quarter of a mile then turn left into a lane which soon loses its surface, signposted 'Langdon Hill ¾', rising steadily. This is a fine walkers' lane,

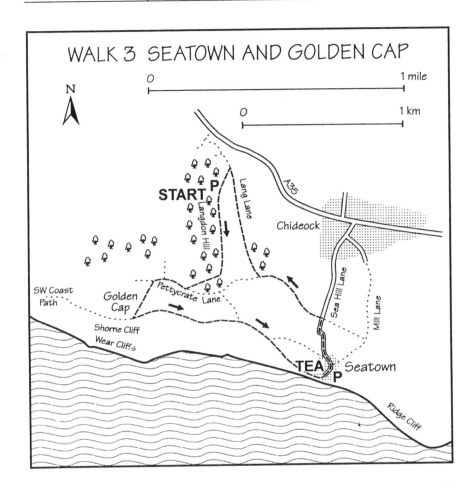

WALK 3 SEATOWN AND GOLDEN CAP

with good views inland over Chideock and of Langdon Hill ahead. Golden Cap is peeping to the left. Another track joins from the right; in a further 200m turn right. This is Langdon Lane, less steep but still rising a little between its flower-girt bankings.

Turn sharp left at a junction, pass a gate, and rise along the access roadway to the car park.

---

4. Eype and West Bay

Length	5 ¼ miles
Summary	Another well-varied walk ranging from the modern holiday ambience of West Bay to the lonely summit of Thornecombe Beacon, with a lovely length of the South West Coast Path in between. Three ascents, none of them long or difficult and generally good tracks underfoot. Nearly one mile on a very minor road.
Car Parking	Large free landscaped car park, with public conveniences and refreshments by the side of the A35 Bridport by-pass, grid reference 451922.
Maps	Ordnance Survey Explorer no. 29, Lyme Regis and Bridport, 1:25,000 or Landranger no. 193, Taunton and Lyme Regis, 1:50,000.

Tea Shop

Eype House Tea Garden is at present a "fair weather" only place. But, subject to local authority consent, a conservatory tea room will soon be open. Meanwhile the garden is sheltered and there is some seating under the veranda. The shop, which is also the reception office for the caravan site, is where you select and order refreshments. Tea, coffee, cold drinks, ice creams, are available. To eat one can choose a cream tea, cakes, sandwiches, and toasted sandwiches – the hot bacon ones are especially good. Pleasing blue and white crockery and pleasant service. Beautiful views.

Open: 9am – 5pm (6pm in high season) every day from Easter to end of October. Tel. 01308 424903.

About the Area

Although Lower Eype straggles for some distance along a minor road which runs from the A35 to the coast, the village still doesn't quite reach the sea. Nestling in its valley, with the church on higher ground above, this is a peaceful place except in high season when the beach at Eype Mouth, with adjacent car park, is a considerable attraction.

The ancient market town of Bridport, first charter 1253, is not much more than a mile from Eype. Although just off the line of this walk, it should be visited for its overall attraction and historic interest. Old buildings include the originally 13th century parish church of St Mary, restored in the mid 19th century, a 16th century building now used as a museum and the Town Hall of 1785. After defeat at Worcester in 1651, the future King Charles II came to Bridport in disguise after failing to escape by sea from Charmouth.

The traditional industry has always been rope making, of great importance in the days when sailing ships needed immense quantities of rope and netting, dating back at least to the time of King John. The layout of Bridport with wide streets and long 'rows' still shows the effect of this industry in shaping the growth of the town.

West Bay has been a port since Roman times and probably before. Subject to periodic damage in great storms, the present harbour was constructed in 1744. It still has minor use and is attractive, although now surrounded by the trappings of a modern holiday resort.

West Bay harbour

The Walk

Leave the car park by the vehicular entrance and turn sharp left, up-hill. In 150m turn right along a very minor road. Proceed generally uphill for a little more than three-quarters of a mile, passing Higher Eype and going straight on at a junction. If you don't like road walking don't despair; this is the only significant length in the circuit and is virtually traffic free.

Just as the road starts to descend, there is a small informal parking place on the left. Turn left here to take a clear track ascending to Eype Down. Follow this quite steeply up the bluebell covered hillside, keeping left as another track joins in less than 200m and soon reaching gorse. At a signposted cross tracks turn right for 'Coast path. Thorncombe Beacon', still rising over well-trodden grass with the view now including Golden Cap, wooded Langdon Hill and Chideock. Thorncombe Beacon soon comes into view ahead, with Seatown and its caravan sites to the right, below.

Pass a waymark on a post and join a more major track. After a gate/stile the path again becomes more minor, rather indistinct over grass, still heading for the Beacon. Keep close to a fence on the left to reach a signposted stile. Cross a path to climb the last few metres direct to the Beacon, where there is still a real beacon, a seat and superb views including the Isle of Portland, reaching far out to sea.

Turn left to commence the steep descent over grass. Particularly in wet weather many will prefer to return inland for a few metres and then turn right to follow the path which descends less steeply. The steep part is quite short, both routes coming together at a signposted stile.

The way to Eype Mouth is straightforward, with a good view of Lower Eype village and its rather isolated church. A little sign advertises the tea gardens and shop in 300m as the path approaches Eype Mouth car park. At the road turn left for a very short distance to reach the refreshments.

After tea return to the South West Coast Path at Eype Mouth and go down the steps to the shingle. Cross the stream on a little bridge and follow the path uphill to the top of West Cliffs, flanked by thrift and sea kale. Bridport is soon in view, as is Colmer's Hill with its distinctive cap of a few trees, near Symondsbury.

Pass a little pond then go through a gate/stile signposted 'Coast path. West Bay ½'. The view of West Bay is now comprehensive. The

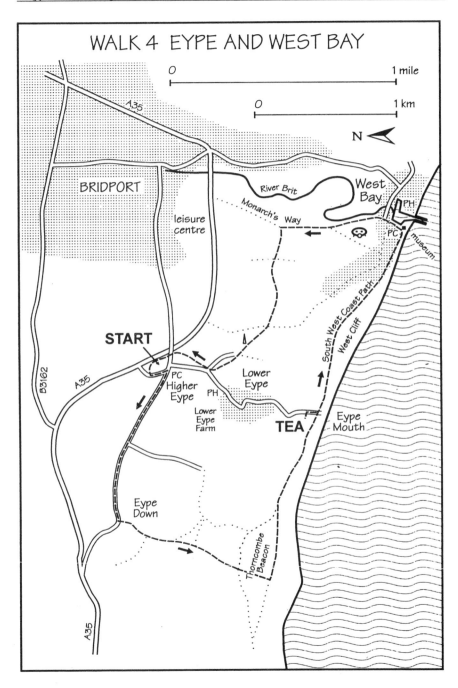

WALK 4 EYPE AND WEST BAY

well-worn grass track goes straight down, via a kissing gate, to the sea front of West Bay. The cliffs on the way down provide a home for considerable numbers of jackdaws.

Walk along the sea front and follow the road round to the left, beside the harbour. Pass to the left of the museum and public conveniences and go through the entrance to Haven Holidays Holiday Park, a large static caravan site. There is a 'Bridport and Y.H.A.' signpost. Walk along the main surfaced drive; at the far end the road turns to the left. Go straight on here. along a waymarked footpath of paving stones. Leave the caravan park at a kissing gate, now labelled as part of the Brit Valley Way.

After a short length of woodland and a waymarked kissing gate/stile, go across the bottom of a large meadow on a good path. To the right the River Brit meanders through the meadows on its last lap to the sea. The next kissing gate has two waymarks; the indicated short cut to the left is not apparent on the ground and it is probably better to continue along the meadow bottom to the next gate.

Turn left here up by the near side of the hedge; the path is only faintly visible on the ground. At the top go through a gap into the next field, where there may be a waymark. Our route is along by the hedge on the left, barely worn. Go over a waymarked double stile at the top, then keep the hedge on the right, still rising, to another waymarked stile, rather overgrown.

Continue along the edge of another field to reach a junction of several paths. Go straight on with a hedge on the left, heading for a communications mast; the path is now well defined, still rising. and there are long views inland. Go through a gate to a surfaced road, crossing to a signposted bridleway to pass close to a house, Rye Combe. The path narrows and is somewhat overgrown.

Continue downhill to reach a public road at a junction. Go up the banking on the right to take a waymarked footpath, well marked across a field to a gate/stile. Turn left along a broad unsurfaced roadway, cross a public road and go over the crash barrier to a waymarked stile. A little path descends through overgrown shrubbery to the car park.

5. Broad Windsor and Pilsdon Pen

Length	6¾ miles
Summary	The village of Broad Windsor is well placed as a base for a walk which includes two of Dorset's highest hills, Pilsdon Pen and Lewesdon Hill. Each has an iron age hill fort. This is quite a demanding walk for its length, with the two ascents plus some awkward farm fields and muddy areas. Care is needed with route finding in one or two places on the Jubilee Trail section.
Car Parking	At Pilsdon Pen there is a roadside parking area sufficient for about 12 vehicles, grid reference 415009 or at the Craft Centre in Broad Windsor there is car parking for customers, grid reference 440024.
Maps	Ordnance Survey Explorer no. 29, Lyme Regis and Bridport, 1:25,000 or Landranger no. 193, Taunton and Lyme Regis, 1:50,000.

Tea Shop

Broadwindsor is a typical village – one shop, one pub, church , and P.O. – all quiet and charming. Just a short distance from the village is the Craft and Design Centre – a somewhat brave enterprise started about seven years ago and, judging from the number of visitors on an "out of main season" Monday morning, apparently successful. Having undertaken one of the more strenuous walks in the book the need for rest and refreshment can be well satisfied here. The main restaurant is superb with beautiful furniture – glass-topped tables and comfy cane chairs with attractive paintings on the walls. If still wearing boots, the conservatory with tiled floor may feel more appropriate for walkers. The food is good. Dishes of the day are displayed on the blackboard and there is a wide choice of sandwiches, scones, and very tempting cakes – the Dorset apple cake is highly recommended. Tea and coffee and cold drinks are all of good quality.
Open: every day from 10am – 5pm from 1st March to 23rd December. Tel. 01308 868362.

Broadwindsor craft centre and tea rooms

About the Area

The substantial village of Broad Windsor has yet another of the local associations with the escape of the unfortunate future King Charles II after his defeat at Worcester in 1651. He spent the night at the George Inn here after fleeing from Charmouth and then Bridport. The village has cottages of the 17th and 18th centuries and a parish church with 12th and 13th century features, including Norman south arcade and font. The fine pulpit is Jacobean.

Close to Broad Windsor are two of Dorset's highest and finest hills, both included in this walk. There is, however, a problem; Pilsdon Pen has long been regarded as the highest in the county, quoted at 908ft. on the old 1" Ordnance Survey map and the metric equivalent of 277m on the brand new Explorer map. But . . . the old map has Lewesdon Hill at 893ft. (272m), whilst the Explorer elevates it to 279m (915ft.) ! A discrepancy of this magnitude does defy explanation. Perhaps local residents have copied the Welsh villagers in a recent film starring Hugh Grant in which a hill quite suddenly became a mountain.

It doesn't, of course, matter. In their very different ways both are fine hills, one long, bare, flat topped and with the brooding presence of a great iron age fort, probably second only to Maiden Castle, whilst the other is heavily wooded, prettier, more intimate, with its lesser iron age fort less apparent.

The Walk

From the Craft Centre walk to the public road and turn left towards the village centre. At the first road junction go downhill on the road-side footpath. Pass the White Lion Inn and the village stores, turning left to 'Axminster'. Stay with this road to the top of a hill, then fork right into a minor lane, Grange Lane, signposted 'Burstock ½.'

You are now on the Monarch's Way; what is fit for a Monarch must be fine for a humble tea shop walker! Blackdown Hill and Pilsdon Pen are in view left, ahead. The latter is our first main objective. Pass Burstock Grange Farm on the left then, at a road junction by Pound Cottage, turn left into an unsurfaced lane, Sheepwash Lane.

At a signpost in a short distance turn right to follow a 'public footpath' sign, again on the Monarch's Way. Go diagonally across a descending field on a well worn track heading for Lower Newnham Farm. Go over a double stile, with a 'Wessex Ridgeway' waymark and continue across the next field. Keep left along a farm track, then left at a waymarked junction in about 60m to go through the farm. Turn right then left to exit along the farm access driveway.

Cross a minor road to continue the ascent of Pilsdon Pen on a broad, stony, track between fences, not quite as shown by the Ordnance Survey. Next is the steepest part of the climb, over grass up to a waymarked post. Turn right to walk past gorse and bluebells to a stile on the left giving access to the top of the hill. Turn left to walk along the broad top to the trig. point at the south-eastern end, accompanied by the unmistakable song of skylarks.

The views from this vantage point seem to include most of west Dorset and south Somerset, including coastal features such as Golden Cap.

Our track leaves the summit steeply downhill by a popular path reaching the road at an obvious gate close to a junction. By the roadside is the parking place which can be used by those wanting refreshments part way round the circuit. The National Trust interpretation board here gives the height of Pilsdon Pen as 300m (984ft.), with a positive claim of highest hill. All very puzzling.

Proceed down the minor road signposted 'Pilsdon and Shave's Cross'. At the large house, Pilsdon Barn, follow the waymark near the entrance.

From this point a short cut can be made by walking down the little road for about three-quarters of a mile instead of leaving it at Pilsdon Barn.

At Pilsdon Barn go between the house and the tennis court, and through a waymarked arch in a hedge. Turn left, go under coniferous trees and to a waymarked stile above an obvious gate. Go over the stile, descend along the edge of a field keeping close to the hedge on the right. Go through a gate on the right and head across the next field to a gap in the far hedge, still descending. Keep the same line to reach a minor road at a gate close to agricultural buildings.

Turn right then, in less than 200m, turn left at a bridleway sign. We are now on the Jubilee Way, unfortunately not as splendid as it sounds and requiring effort and care over the next mile or so. Head across a muddy area to a waymarked gate and diagonally across a field to a waymarked gate in the top corner. Pilsdon Manor is to the right.

Go through the gate and follow the waymark, with the hedge on the right. Go through an unmarked gap on the right and turn left to continue beside the hedge, downhill. Note that there has been a legal diversion of the footpath hereabouts. Despite the diversion in his favour the farmer has ploughed much too close to the edge of the field. After the waymarked gate at the bottom bear right to follow the field boundary on the diverted section, again ploughed too close in places. To the right is a lovely little valley, full of bluebells in Spring.

Reach a minor road and go straight across into what appears to be an old lane. After a waymarked gate cross a swampy area and then a cultivated field, with Laverstock Farm to the left. A stile gives access to the farm road. There may be diversions here; if so, follow the arrows. Otherwise, go across and bear left to the corner of the field and a rough, stony, roadway.

Go over a waymarked stile on the right and take a clear track across another cultivated field to a waymarked stile. Continue by bearing right across a meadow to head for a small wooded valley, entered over a waymarked stile. The path through the wood is clear,

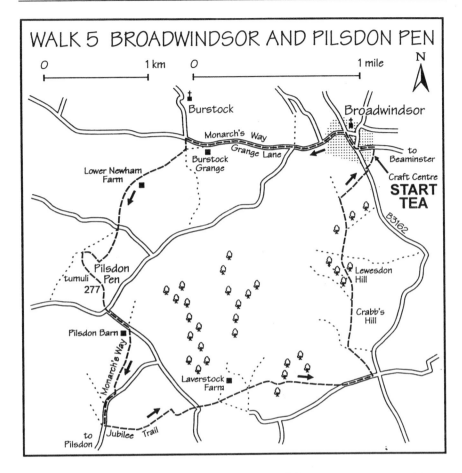

WALK 5 BROADWINDSOR AND PILSDON PEN

0 ___ 1 km   0 ___ 1 mile   N

Burstock

Broadwindsor

Monarch's Way

Grange Lane

Burstock Grange

Lower Newham Farm

to Beaminster

Craft Centre

START
TEA

B3162

Pilsdon Pen
tumuli 277

Lewesdon Hill

Crabb's Hill

Pilsdon Barn

Monarch's Way

Laverstock Farm

to Pilsdon

Jubilee Trail

with a steep little climb on the far side of the stream, crossed by a plank bridge.

Exit at a waymarked stile and bear left, uphill, to a farm gate. The right of way angles to the right across this field but to keep close to the left-hand boundary may well provide easier walking. In either case a gate at the top gives access to a public road. Lewesdon Hill, the next objective, is the high ground to the left.

Turn left to walk along the road. Just before the junction with the B3162, go through a waymarked gate on the left to follow a track across a cultivated field to another waymarked gate and carry on by the hedge on the right to an exit gate and a concreted track.

Turn left along the track and then right in 30m at a gate to take the bridleway rising directly to the top of the hill. Bear left at a fork. This is a lovely track within a narrow tree belt, rich in beeches, with the most incredible display of bluebells in Spring, and with occasional views back to Pilsdon Pen.

The top of the hill, owned by the National Trust, is a very attractive place. As the track forks, go right to descend towards Broad Windsor, soon crossing a lane-like bridleway to a waymarked stile. Keep close to the hedge on the left along a fairly clear path, then straight across a field to a gate in the bottom boundary. Bear right to a waymarked gate and along a field boundary.

The track towards the edge of the village is well worn over grass. Reach the public road and turn left. In 40m turn right into Redlands Lane and pass through modern housing development direct to the car park.

6. Beaminster and Stoke Abbott

Length	5 ½ miles
Summary	A walk linking the little market town of Beaminster with the quiet village of Stoke Abbot, one of Dorset's prettiest, passing through lovely countryside, including part of the Wessex Ridgeway. Apart from the odd cultivated field, lanes and good paths throughout; a very short distance is on a minor road.
Car Parking	The preferred parking place is the central pay and display car park, with public conveniences, in Beaminster, grid reference 481014. To enjoy refreshments part way round the circuit, find a roadside space at Stoke Abbott.
Maps	Ordnance Survey Explorer no. 29, Lyme Regis and Bridport, 1:25,000 or Landranger no. 193, Taunton and Lyme Regis, 1:50,000.

Tea Shop

"The Tea Shoppe" in Church Street is an example of an authentic English tea room; small, cosy, and comforting – particularly after a good walk when a cup of tea is so welcome.

Leaf tea is served here with strainer provided – there really is a difference in leaf as against tea bags – what a pity that more cafés don't take that small amount of extra trouble. To eat there are salads, omelettes, toasted sandwiches, even chips, as well as a choice of home made cakes and absolutely superb scones. Traditional roast lunches are served on Sundays but reservations are requested. Open: 10.30am – 5pm, Sundays 12noon – 5pm. Closed every Tuesday. Tel. 01308 862513.

About the Area

Just a little way off the beaten track, the tiny market town of Beaminster sits in a rich valley among the hills of west Dorset. Shops and inns cluster around the Square, with its prominent market cross. Disastrous fires, two in the 17th century and one in the 18th century, have ensured that, apart from the church and an adjacent almshouse, there are few buildings of real antiquity. However, there are many Georgian houses and the overall impression is of a nice old town.

The church is largely of the 15th century, with a 13th century arcade and a Norman font bowl. Highly regarded is the tower, rich in sculptures and notorious as the place where several local people were hung following the Monmouth rebellion.

Less than a mile along the Bridport road is Parnham House, a Tudor gem, open to the public on Sundays, Tuesdays, Wednesdays, Thursdays and Bank Holidays from April to October.

Beautifully situated among the hills, Stoke Abbott is a trim village with neat thatch and stone cottages surrounded by colourful gardens. The church has Norman features and the New Inn provides refreshments. Nearby Whaddon Hill has the site of a Roman fort, probably built as part of a defensive chain by Vespasian in the early years of the occupation and used only for a comparatively short time. From this hill back to Beaminster is a fine part of the Wessex Ridgeway.

The Walk

From Beaminster car park walk back to the market square and across to Church Street, heading for the church. Turn left into St Mary's Well Street. forking right as the street ends by a stream. The roadway soon loses its surface. At a kissing gate the waymarks include 'Brit Valley Circular Walk'.

Leave the broad track at a waymarked post for 'Netherbury 1' to follow a narrow footpath rising gently across grass. Go through a kissing gate and straight on across a large rising meadow. The back of Parnham House is visible to the left. Fork right at a waymarked gate/stile. This is now the Hardy Way and the Jubilee Trail. In less than quarter of a mile go over a stile on the right, signposted 'Jubilee Trail' but with no visible wear on the ground.

Angle up the hillside, over grass, heading for a clump of six mixed beech and horse chestnut trees and a waymarked stile in the hedge beyond. Cross an unsurfaced lane and go over another waymarked stile. Cross a cultivated field on the same line to a waymarked gate and a fork at the near end of a footbridge.

Turn right here along a path by the stream, soon reaching another footbridge. Cross this bridge and leave the woodland. The way con-

WALK 6 BEAMINSTER AND STOKE ABBOTT

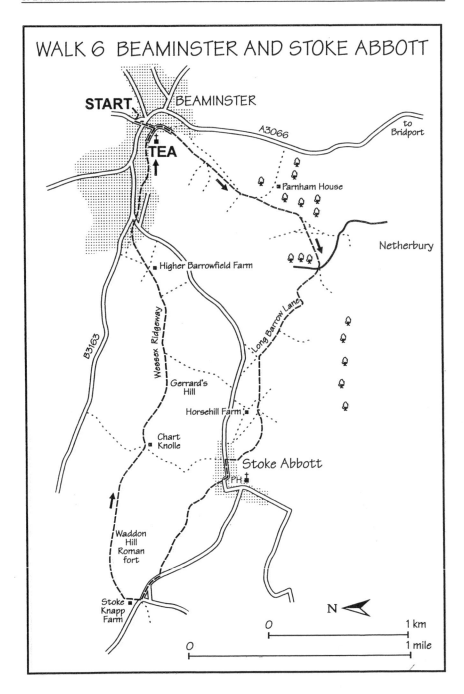

START BEAMINSTER

A3066

to
Bridport

TEA

Parnham House

Netherbury

Higher Barrowfield Farm

Wessex Ridgeway

Long Barrow Lane

B3163

Gerrard's
Hill

Horsehill Farm

Chart
Knolle

Stoke Abbott

PH

Waddon
Hill
Roman
fort

Stoke
Knapp
Farm

N

0   1 km

0   1 mile

tinues up a large rising field, aiming half way between the hedge on the left and a solitary tree. At the top of the field go along a rather overgrown lane, soon bearing right along Long Barrow Lane, fringed by the ubiquitous ramsoms and red campion.

In just under half a mile go over a waymarked stile on the left, across the corner of a field to another two stiles and then diagonally across a small field to a waymarked stile to continue along a visible path through rough grass and nettles. Cross a footbridge over a stream and go across the corner of the next field to a gate/stile.

Cross a muddy lane into woodland opposite. The next section is a delightful woodland path. Leave the wood at a footbridge and keep close to the lower edge of a meadow. Thirty metres before the end of the meadow turn right over a stile, then a footbridge, and climb the opposite bank, bearing left to a stile and a passage through to the road in Stoke Abbott.

Turn left to the New Inn and a house with sub-tropical palms in the garden. Turn right opposite the inn at a 'public footpath' sign-post to follow an old sunken lane, rising gently. At the end of the lane go over a waymarked stile and straight across a huge rising meadow. The route is not very clear on the ground; go along the raised spine to the exit stile at the far top end.

An awkwardly steep little descent leads to a minor road. Turn right, pass a cottage at a junction, and reach a more important road. In 30m turn right at a 'public footpath. Wessex Way' sign to go through the back of a farm to a waymarked gate. Follow a wheel-tracked route uphill; Whaddon Hill to the right is the site of the Roman fort. Climb steadily to two farm gates, with a waymark in between. The better route is to take that on the right.

Continue to another gate, pass an old quarry, and go downhill over grass. Gerrard's Hill, with its crown of trees, is in view as our next objective. Go through a waymarked gate and approach a size-able property, Chart Knolle, which sits astride the saddle linking the two hills. Follow the waymarked round to the left of the property, turning right to return to the original course immediately after pass-ing the buildings. Head for the top of the hill, over short grass, with a hedge on the left. The ascent is comparatively easy, going through a gate to reach the summit, with its trees and a trig. point. The excel-lent views include Beaminster.

Continue along the same path to descend the ridge, over two stiles and then down a large meadow, heading for a decrepit tree, where there are waymarks on a post. Descend a steep bank to a stile and footbridge at the bottom boundary of the field. Rise through a plantation of young trees, go over two stiles and round the end of a farm building with a 'Brit Valley Circular Walk' waymark.

Go straight on across a field to a squeezer stile to reach a residential road, Halfacre Lane. Turn right, join a more important road, and turn left. In 30m turn right along a signposted path with a stream on the right. Keep straight on over the occasional stile to reach Shorts Lane and then Church Street, bearing left up to the tea shop, the market square and the car park.

---

7. Mangerton Mill

Length	3 miles
Summary	A short easy walk, initially by the side of the tiny Mangerton River, from the mill to the fringe of Bradpole, with the return over the adjacent hill top. Most of the necessary ascent is on a very minor road. The footpaths are not all well-defined but some mud is the only difficulty underfoot.
Car Parking	Mangerton Mill has a car park for customers, grid reference 490958. Otherwise, there are just occasional roadside spaces.
Maps	Ordnance Survey Explorer no. 117, Cerne Abbas and Bere Regis, 1:25,000 or Landranger no. 193, Taunton and Lyme Regis, 1:50,000.

Tea Shop

The complex at Mangerton Mill is fascinating. Apart from the walk, one can while away happy hours looking at the exhibits of mechanical power restored and demonstrated by a charming enthusiast, visit the numerous craft rooms where unique and beautiful goods at reasonable prices may prove irresistible, or stroll round the trout lake and along the riverside path. The main object after the walk is the well earned refreshment at the mill house. Inside is a pleasantly furnished café whilst outside there is a sunny sheltered terrace – all very relaxing. From mid-morning onwards one can enjoy coffee, lunch, or afternoon tea. During the period noon to 2pm cooked meals such as chilli con carne with salad, bacon baps, beans on toast, are available. Afternoon temptations are the "Dorset Cream Tea" or, for something less sweet, the "Mangerton Tea" may appeal – this offers a cheese scone with butter, slice of home-made tea bread, and a pot of tea. The "Country Tea" comprises cucumber sandwiches, slice of cake, and tea. Of course one can choose individual items from the menu – just order at the counter and food is brought to your table.

Open: Good Friday to the end of October from 11am – 5.30pm. every day but closed on Mondays except Bank Holidays. Tel. 01308 485224.

About the Area

Mangerton Mill is the hub of an interesting little visitor complex, with craft premises and a collection of vintage engines supplementing the 17th century working water mill itself. It is readily accessible about 3 miles north of Bridport, signposted from the A3066 Bridport to Beaminster road.

Mangerton Mill

The Walk

Leave the mill along the access drive and turn left at the public road. As the road kinks to the right, turn left immediately after a modern house at a gate with waymark and a 'Bradpole' sign. Proceed along the left-hand boundary of the field, and into the next field.

Turn right to aim for the far left corner, beside the river, where there is a rudimentary stile, with waymark. The path continues, not always very distinct, more or less close to the river. Occasional waymarked stiles confirm the route, which has some boggy ground.

On reaching a small copse, look out for a waymarked stile on the left, pass through the mini wood, exiting by a plank bridge and stile.

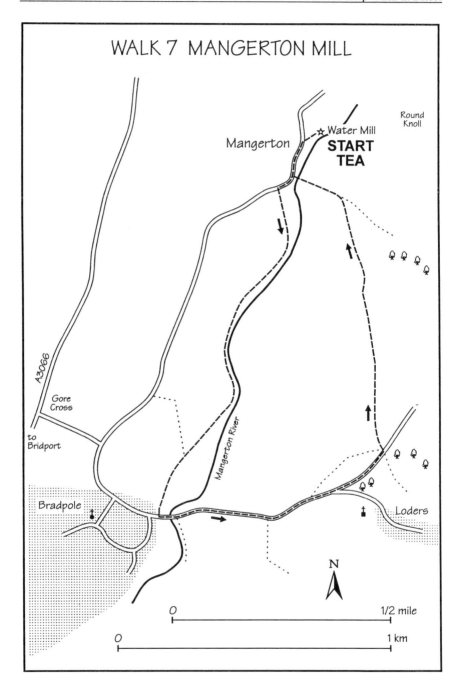

WALK 7 MANGERTON MILL

Round
Knoll

☆ Water Mill

Mangerton

**START
TEA**

A3066

Gore
Cross

to
Bridport

Mangerton River

Bradpole

Loders

N

0   1/2 mile

0   1 km

The waymark tells us that we are on part of the Brit Valley Circular Walk. Continue across a meadow to a waymarked gateway, with a fair sized farm to the right. Bear right to a stile opposite and continue the same line.

Go through a waymarked gate on the approach to Metz Farm, then through the farm to a minor public road. Turn left, cross the river, and rise steadily. At the crest of the hill turn left for ' West Milton. Nettlecombe' on a surfaced lane in a deep cutting.

Just before the top of the road turn left into an unmade track with a 'Church Farm' sign. The track is cattle-churned for some distance. After a gateway, keep straight on with a hedge on the right, Go over two rudimentary waymarked stiles behind an electricity pylon and, a little way further, go through the hedge on the right into a large, descending, field.

According to the Ordnance Survey, the right of way is diagonally across, but it is probably better to stay close to the left-hand edge and then to bear right along a grassy shelf at the bottom end. From the shelf turn left to descend the bank and join a bridleway at the foot for the last 150m to a farm gate and the public road.

Turn right at the road to return to the mill driveway and car park.

---

8. Burton Bradstock and Shipton Gorge

Length   6 miles

Summary   Burton Bradstock and Shipton Gorge villages are combined into a
                circular walk by the use of field paths, lanes, and a section of the South
                West Coast Path. It has to be said that not all rights of way across
                agricultural land are clear on the ground and some sections may be a
                little overgrown. However, the waymarking is generally good and the
                rolling countryside is always attractive. A little more than half a mile is
                along minor roads.

Car Parking   Free car park serving Cogden Beach just off the main Burton
                Bradstock to Abbotsbury road, a little more than a mile east of Burton
                Bradstock, grid reference 502886. To have a vehicle close to the sea,
                the National Trust (pay) car park at Burton Beach is spacious and has
                good facilities including public conveniences.

Maps   Ordnance Survey Outdoor Leisure no. 15, Purbeck and South Dorset,
                1:25,000 or Landrangers nos. 193, Taunton and Lyme Regis and 194,
                Dorchester and Weymouth, 1:50,000.

Tea Shop

Bridge Cottage Stores proudly and justifiably displays press cuttings
of being chosen Dorset Best Village Shop for 1994 – if the competi-
tion is still held this shop must be a strong contender for repeated
success. Bridge Cottage offers just about everything from groceries
to lottery tickets and reasonably priced bed and breakfast accommo-
dation in en-suite rooms. However, it is the tea-room that is of particular interest to the walker. Thirsty ramblers can select from a choice
of teas and from various blends of coffee – the latter with unlimited
refills! Cold drinks include citrus presse, elderflower presse and,
unusually, Lucozade. The Dorset apple cake, which is served warm,
and the chocolate shortbread are definitely not for slimmers and
whilst feeling self-indulgent try the ice cream topped with clotted
cream – absolutely delicious. Should savoury rather than sweet ap-

peal, sample the local speciality snack of Dorset Knob with Blue Vinny cheese and pickle or "Tiddy Oggies" which are pasties made with minced beef and vegetables.
Open: 8am to 5.30pm (7pm in main holiday season) every day except Christmas Day. Tel. 01308 897222

About the Area

The substantial village of Burton Bradstock is close to Bridport, about 3 miles along the B3157, Abbotsbury, road. Apart from the store/tea shop, the best of the village is on the inland side of this road. Old cottages, two inns and numerous little streets happily combine in this most attractive place. Most of the parish church is of 14th/15th century origin, much restored at the end of the 19th century, with a central tower rising from panelled arches.

The stony rampart of Chesil Beach extends for several miles from Burton Bradstock to Portland.

The inland village of Shipton Gorge is served only by minor roads. Largely residential, with some pretty cottages, this pleasant village has a church with a perpendicular tower and a 13th century font with heptagonal bowl.

Shipton Gorge

As well as appearing to be a rest home/graveyard for large numbers of clapped out vehicles, Cogden Farm houses a most unusual car hire organisation with powerful vintage sports cars.

The Walk

Leave the car park and turn right along the road for about 200m, by a fair margin the least attractive part of this circuit. Turn left into the drive to Cogden Farm, home of Chesil Speedsters and much other automobilia. Fork right as the drive separates and go through several gates to the right of the farm, turning left behind the buildings to return to the original line.

Leave the farm by a stony uphill track to a gate giving access to a large meadow. Bear right at about 45 degrees here – there is no path on the ground but aim for the far right corner to an exit via a waymarked stile. Cross into the next field and turn left to stay close to the hedge on a faint track.

The flat capped top ahead is Shipton Hill, crowned by an Iron Age fort. Go over another, rather overgrown, stile and continue the same line along the edge of another field to reach a minor road through two farm gates. Turn left for 40m and then right, along a road signposted 'Shipton Gorge'. Cross the River Bride and rise past Bredy Farm to a junction. Turn left to pass Bredy Cottages, cross a stream, and turn right immediately after Brook Cottage.

A broad, rough, farm track leads to a waymarked gate. Continue along a well marked track close to a stream on the right. At the second waymarked farm gate on the right, turn down to cross the stream on a few easy stepping stones. Turn left and stay close to the stream along the bottom of a field, skirting below Cathole Copse to a waymarked gate. Continue as before, to an exit by the right corner and a defined path through undergrowth.

Cross a stone slab bridge over the stream and then go straight across a field, with Shipton Gorge visible on the hill ahead. Make for a gap in the hedge ahead and continue along a farm track in preference to the Ordnance Survey line a few metres to the left. At a cross tracks either continue past agricultural buildings to join the public road at one end of the village (there is no apparent right of way) or turn left to rejoin the proper right of way at a stile on the right in about 100m

Go over the stile, cross a small field to a stone slab bridge and stile

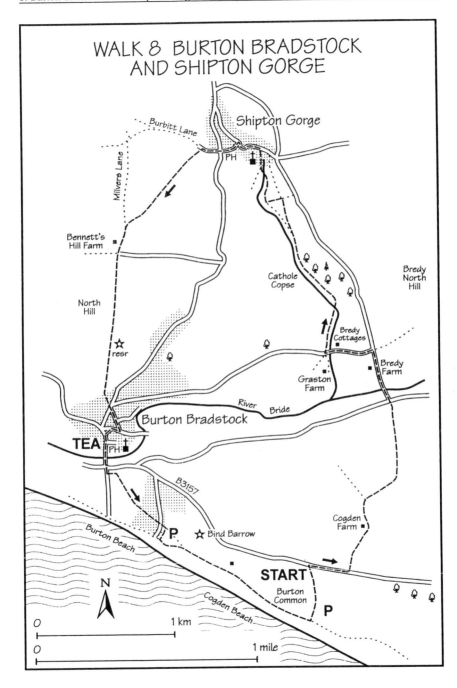

WALK 8 BURTON BRADSTOCK AND SHIPTON GORGE

to head straight for the church up a rising field of buttercups. Go to the angle of the churchyard wall and follow a footpath over two old stone slab stiles down to the village street.

Near to the telephone box is the base of what appears to be an old cross.

Turn left, pass a road junction, and go uphill. Go across the next road junction; the New Inn is to the right here. Continue along an unmade track for about 150m and go over a waymarked stile on the left. There are now 5 fields to cross, from waymarked stile to waymarked stile in each case. At first the path is quite distinct over grass; field by field it becomes progressively less so, but the line is held fairly straight throughout.

Leave the last field by a gate into a farm lane. Turn left, uphill, passing Bennett's Hill Farm to the right. At a junction turn right, then immediately left through a gate with blue bridleway waymark. Keep close to the hedge on the left and go over the hill through a waymarked gate.

Burton Bradstock now comes into view as the track goes downhill, still close to the hedge on the left; there is a disused reservoir in an adjacent field. After a gate the track is down what appears to be a very old lane, part overgrown and muddy. Obviously many walkers have diverted to the right for a much easier route alongside the lane. At the bottom the track becomes broad and easy, soon reaching a road at the edge of Burton Bradstock.

Turn right and then left in a few metres, to Middle Street. Reach the main road either by Donkey Lane or by Mill Street. Turn left at the main road to walk to the tea shop.

Turn left out of the tea shop. As the road bends by the filling station, head into Cliff Road, turn left up steps behind the buildings, with a 'to the beach' signpost, and follow a pleasant path heading for the back of the beach buildings. The National Trust car park is reached via two kissing gates.

Walk through the car park, with its various facilities and turn left at the coast path. The way is obvious, keeping close to the coast, low cliffs and a shingle/sand beach. Pass a large static caravan site to reach the National Trust Cogden area, rich in sea kale and the delicate colour of thrift.

As the path joins the shingle of the beach, turn left, uphill, to follow a broad track direct to the car park, passing two gates and N.T. information boards.

9. Abbotsbury and The Hill Fort

Length	5½ miles
Summary	A wonderful combination of part of the sea coast, Chesil Beach, and a downland scarp facing the sea. Largely on parts of the South West Coast Path, this walk is excellent underfoot. Long but not difficult ascent from the sea to 215m (706ft.)
Car Parking	Back of beach car park with public conveniences, accessed by a cul de sac road leaving the main road half a mile to the west of Abbotsbury, grid reference 560846.
Maps	Ordnance Survey Outdoor Leisure no. 15, Purbeck and South Dorset, 1:25,000 or Landranger no. 194, Dorchester and Weymouth, 1:50,000

Tea Shop

Tea in an old Dorset farmhouse – delightful! East Farm serves classic teas – cream or plain; the English afternoon tea includes lovely cucumber sandwiches and home made cake. Also available are cheese and pickle sandwiches and Dorset apple cake served with cream. Decor is interesting – the furniture is farmhouse style with cheerful red and white gingham tablecloths and matching chair seat cushions. The two tea rooms are positively cluttered with crafts available to purchase. A very special attraction is "George" the talkative parrot – reputedly about ten years old and very chatty indeed. No need to converse just sit and listen to George! Bed and breakfast is also available.
Open: Easter to end of October every day, 2pm – 5pm. Tel. 01305 871363

About the Area

The many attractions of Abbotsbury are described in walk no. 10. An important part of the lovely setting of this popular village is the enclosing ridge of high ground to the north, which maintains a height of around 200m (656ft.) for several miles, with a prominent hill fort, Abbotsbury Castle, at the highest part (215m. – 706ft.). The south facing scarp has the inland variation of the South West Coast Path along the top.

The Dorset coast, near Abbotsbury

The Walk

Leave the car park at the right-hand corner, by the public conveniences, to follow a narrow tarmac road, close to the sea. Pass Castle Hill Cottages. The views along the coast are extensive. In a little more than 1 mile turn right at a stone sign 'Bridleway Hill Fort 1½'. This is the start of the long continuous ascent. Head uphill to the large farmstead of East Bexington, on a good track along the edge of a field, then through a gate, to pass to the right of the farm, before bearing left as indicated by a 'Hill Fort' signpost near the fence above.

Exit through a gate and go to a second gate, then diagonally right to rise across a field towards a tree-flanked house. Go over a stile and round to the right to continue the upward slog close to a hedge/fence. Go over a stile at the top and follow a good path among brambles. Fork right in less than 100m at an 'Abbotsbury and Hill Fort' signpost.

The gorse-clad slope is now at its steepest as the top of Tulks Hill

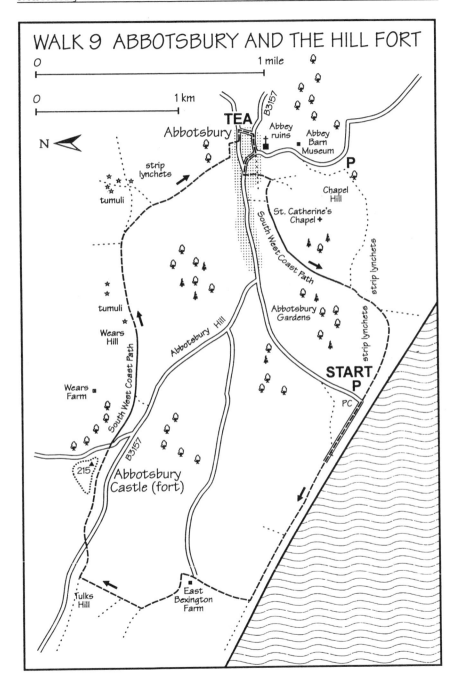

WALK 9 ABBOTSBURY AND THE HILL FORT

draws near. Turn right at a signpost 'Hardy Monument 4½, Osmington Mills 15'. The hill fort is now clearly in view ahead. The splendid views include coastal and inland Dorset, with the village of Punchknowle prominent to the left.

The path reaches the main road, crossed diagonally at gates/stiles, with the contradictory waymark 'inland coast path'. Head uphill to the top of the fort, interesting if hardly a Maiden Castle, and proceed to the trig. point for the most extensive views.

Continue along the ridge, a superb route over close cropped grass and cross a minor road. After passing high above small ponds turn right at an 'Abbotsbury' signpost and descend towards the village, with a bird's eye view. Initially the path is rather faint on the ground, but it soon becomes entirely clear, passing some outcropping chalk and through several waymarked farm gates to head straight for the village

Go through a gate on the left into a sunken lane before reaching the edge of Abbotsbury. Turn left, then right, to the tea shop.

After the tea shop, turn left to go to the village street. Turn right and walk along to Chapel Lane (about 250m), turning left to go towards St Catherine's Chapel (as in walk no. 10). At a farm building bear right along a broad track descending gently towards the sea, with St Catherine's Chapel on its mound above. At a gate and junction bear left towards the sea, still on a fine track.

At a signpost go right to 'West Bexington 3 Tropical Gardens 1'. The remarkable Chesil Beach is close on the left and there are pebbles underfoot for a short distance before the car park is reached.

10. Abbotsbury and St Catherine's Chapel

Length	1½ miles.
Summary	A very easy short walk readily combined with visits to any of Abbotsbury's several attractions and/or general appreciation of a fine village. The ascent of Chapel Hill is at a gentle gradient.
Car Parking	Village car park at entrance to village on Portesham Road. Modest charge. Grid reference 579853.
Maps	Ordnance Survey Outdoor Leisure no. 15, Purbeck and South Dorset, 1:25,000 or Landranger no. 194, Dorchester and Weymouth, 1:50,000.

Tea Shop

The Abbey House is so beautiful and one is very aware of walking gear when approaching but Maureen Cooke, the owner, is very pleased to welcome walkers. However, if having tea indoors it would be courteous to remove cagoules etc. and to leave boots in the porch of this splendid house – the decor is superb. The tea garden provides a peaceful environment with views of the delightful countryside around Abbotsbury. There are tables on the lawn and some under the arbour – it is all most attractive. The Abbey House is open for lunch and offers a tempting menu of cooked dishes. For tea there is Dorset apple cake – served warm with clotted cream, toasted teacakes, good selection of cakes, or the inclusive tea of scones, jam, and cream. Drinks offered are coffee, tea, Earl Grey tea, cold milk, and fruit juices. Very friendly service.
Open: for lunches and teas from 12noon – 5pm. every day from Easter to October. The Abbey House is also a popular guest house – reservations needed to avoid disappointment. Tel. 01305 871330.

About the Area

Abbotsbury is without doubt one of the most charming of Dorset's stone built villages, nestling in a sheltered valley close to the sea.

Parts of the Benedictine Abbey of St Peter, dating from the early part of the 11th century, have survived the general destruction of the Reformation. Ironically, a manor house built with much of the stone from the dismantled Abbey was itself destroyed by an explosion during a minor battle at the time of the Civil War. The most impressive survival from the Abbey is the great tithe barn, of about 1400, This building measures no less than 83m. by 9.5m.

Adjacent is the 14th century parish church of St Nicholas, also involved in the Civil War conflict when it was defended by supporters of the King. Two bullet holes in the back of the pulpit remain as evidence of those troubled times. A conical mound beside the village, with prominent medieval lynchets on its east side, is capped by St Catherine's Chapel, prime destination of this walk. Built by the monks of the Abbey, this chapel was dedicated to St Catherine of Alexandria, patron saint of spinsters. The structure is still sound, including a stone vaulted roof, and the stripped out interior has interesting information boards, including a spinster's prayer for a husband.

The west end of the West Fleet, a large salt water lagoon, has been home to large numbers of swans for many centuries. Now an organised visitor attraction with facilities, the swannery is open daily from late March to the end of October, from 10am to 6pm. The breeding season in spring is a prime visitor time.

The ancient tithe barn has been adapted into a 'Children's Farm', open daily from Easter to the end of October from 10am to 6pm and at weekends only in winter.

Abbotsbury's other main attraction is the Sub Tropical Garden, situated on the cul de sac road which is the access to the car park in walk no. 9. Open daily all the year round, other than the three main days at Christmas/New Year, from 10am to 6pm during March to November and from 10am to 4pm in winter.

Combined tickets for these three major attractions can be purchased at a discounted price.

The Walk

Leave the car park and turn left along the village street. Go round right then left bends, then turn left at Chapel Lane, with a 'St Catherine's Chapel' signpost. The chapel on its mound is unmistakable ahead.

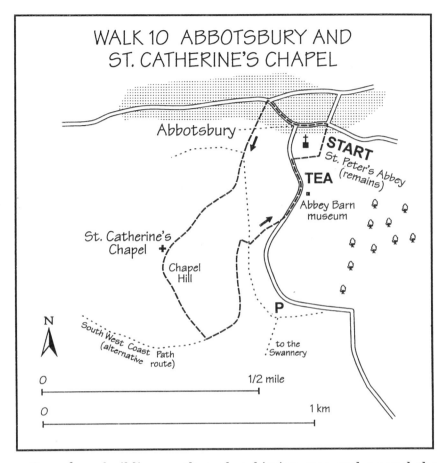

WALK 10 ABBOTSBURY AND ST. CATHERINE'S CHAPEL

By a farm building go through a kissing gate and ascend the well-used path to the chapel. The inside is worth a visit and the mound makes a good viewpoint.

Leave the chapel by going over the stile at the rear; there is a sign-post a few metres to the left. Continue along the 'permissive path' towards the sea, bearing a little to the left to descend over the old lynchets to another signpost and a junction with a variant of the South West Coast Path. The extensive views include much of Chesil Beach, the Isle of Portland and the swannery.

Go left towards a stile but, before the stile, turn left again to a waymarked gate/stile. The path now goes through a small wooded area to reach a waymarked stile. A little way further, turn right,

Abbotsbury

down a bank, cross a stream by a bridge, and follow a signpost towards the swannery, joining a tarmac road after two more stiles.

Turn left, uphill, soon reaching the tithe barn. After passing the barn turn right at a 'village' signpost. Turn left up towards the church and a surviving piece of Abbey wall. The tea shop is on the right and the car park is a little way further.

11. Upwey and
The Hardy Monument

Length   9 miles

Summary   Allow plenty of time for this largely downland walk, which combines a
              considerable length of the Jubilee Way with the inland version of the
              South West Coast Path. Apart from a few awkward fields on the
              Jubilee Way after Upwey, the paths are good and the ascent is not
              excessive. The monument stands on Black Down at a height of 239m.
              (784ft,).

Car Parking   Large free car park by the Hardy Monument, accessed by the minor
              road from Martinstown to Abbotsbury, grid reference 612877.

Maps   Ordnance Survey Outdoor Leisure no. 15, Purbeck and South Dorset,
              1:25,000 or Landranger no. 194, Dorchester and Weymouth, 1:50,000.

Tea Shop

When we first heard of Upwey Wishing Well Water Garden it con-
jured up visions of a large commercial enterprise; the reality is quite
different. For over a hundred years it has been fashionable for people to make the excursion to Upwey to take tea and to make a wish;
although the well provided water for the village it has always had ro-
mantic associations. At one period ladies were employed as
"glass-givers" issuing the glasses and explaining to visitors how to
make a wish. It was even visited by Thomas Hardy and his novel
"The Trumpet Major" is set in Upwey.

Part way round this long walk it is rewarding to arrive in the village and to enjoy well-earned refreshments at this delightful tea
shop and garden. The tea room is large, bright, and cheerful. Service
is most pleasant – the ladies certainly appear to enjoy their work.
Light lunches are served such as ploughman's, sandwiches are
available with various fillings including Portland crab or Upwey
trout. The Wishing Well Tea comprises scones with butter, cream,
jam, and a slice of cake, whilst the English Afternoon Tea includes
cucumber sandwiches and cakes. Coffee, speciality teas, lemonade,

and many other drinks are available. Selection of delicious cakes –
lemon drizzle, sticky date, coffee sponge and many others. This is
without doubt a tea shop not to be missed - customers may also enjoy their tea sitting in the lovely garden. There is no charge to visit
the famous well but donations for charity are invited.
Open: 10.30am - 6pm every day from Easter to 30th September. Tel.
01305 814470/812262

About the Area

Upwey is an attractive village strung along the B3159 to the west of
the Dorchester to Weymouth main road, only just escaping being en-
gulfed in the northern residential expansion of Weymouth. The
15th century church, with modern clerestory, has a tower with pin-
nacles and gargoyles and other interesting features.

However, the village's fame rests securely on the wishing well –
not any old pseudo wishing well designed just to collect money for
good causes, but a real live well sitting over a spring which is the
headwater of the River Wey. There is a remarkable issue of about 1.5
million gallons per day in summer and more in winter, at a steady
temperature of 10.5 degrees Celsius (51 degrees F.). This ready made
river flows for only 5 or 6 miles to the sea at Weymouth.

Following at least one visit by King George III, in 1798, the well became extremely popular as a tourist excursion in Victorian and Ed-
wardian times, using the Upwey Halt railway station and
charabancs for mass transport. The Prince of Wales (later, briefly,
King Edward VIII) was another distinguished visitor in 1923. It is
also recorded that there was a tea garden by the well more than 100
years ago, so our recommendation here will almost certainly be the
oldest tea shop site in the book (and possibly any other tea shop
book!). The present advice for wishing at the well is to drink a little
of the water before throwing the remainder over the left shoulder.
Without assurance that the water purity meets the demanding present day standards, some might be wary about following the first part
of this advice.

During the past 100 years or so, a water garden has been developed by the well. Small but attractive, this garden now has the outdoor tables of the adjacent tea shop. This little complex is still a
considerable visitor attraction.

Two hundred metres downstream is a large former water-powered mill sitting by the side of the newly emerged river. This was the model for the mill in Thomas Hardy's novel 'The Trumpet Major'.

The impressive Hardy Monument is magnificently located in a commanding position on Black Down and is in the care of the National Trust. It was erected in 1844 in commemoration of Vice Admiral Sir Thomas Masterman Hardy, Nelson's Flag Captain at the battle of Trafalgar, of 'kiss me Hardy' fame as Nelson lay dying. There is access to the top of the monument, limited to weekends, early April to late September. Hardy's home was at nearby Portesham.

The wishing well, Upwey

The Walk

Walk down to the road; a little track to the right cuts off a corner. Descend the road as far as a parking lay-by on the left. Opposite this lay-by turn right along a broad track signposted 'Inland Coast Path. Osmington 10'. The track rises at first but soon descends among gorse. This part of S.W.C.P is very easy to follow, passing a junction with the Jubilee Trail, close to the top of Bronkham Hill

At a signposted junction keep straight on for 'Inland route east' The path keeps close to the top of a broad ridge, with occasional tumuli and shake holes for those with an eye for historic features. The occasional waymarked gate confirms the route, which so far is entirely straightforward. Go across a concrete farm road and continue.

The path is now along the edge of a cultivated field, with plenty of space and is obviously well-used.

Stay with 'Inland route east' at a signposted junction, but at the next signpost go to a waymarked gate on the left for 'Bincombe. Osmington', pass tumuli, and continue the previous line, still on the 'Inland route'. Upwey and the large built-up areas north of Weymouth can now be seen. Pass a communications mast and continue to the public road.

Cross over the road and follow the coast path, a stony farm track along the edge of a field. At a signpost 'bridleway to Upwey ¾', turn right. Be careful here; the obvious track just beyond a wall diverts too far to the east. The angle of the signpost gives a better line, soon descending along the bottom of a shallow valley and then bearing right to a gate close to the junction of two public roads. The farmstead of Bayard Dairy should be well away to the left.

Join the road and turn left to descend to Upwey. The church can be seen to the right just before reaching the Wishing Well.

Leave the Wishing Well by the adjacent signposted footpath up to a waymarked gate/stile – 'Jubilee Trail'. Bear right, past the end of a house, and continue rising, through woodland. This track can be muddy in wet weather. Go over a waymarked stile and along the bottom edge of a cultivated field, the gradient soon levelling. Despite the line shown by the Ordnance Survey, keep to the bottom edge of the next field.

The Hardy Monument is soon in view – quite a way still to go – and views to the sea open up to the left. Go over a waymarked stile and across a field on a marked path to reach a gate and a surfaced farm roadway. Go straight across, at first over uncultivated ground. Keep the same line, go over a waymarked double stile, and continue over grazing land at the top of Friar Waddon Hill, bearing to the right of power pylons to descend to a stile giving access to a minor road.

Turn left and go down the Corton entrance drive for 30m. Turn right, over a stile with a 'public footpath' sign. Contour over rough grass above the farm, which has a tiny church/chapel, looking out

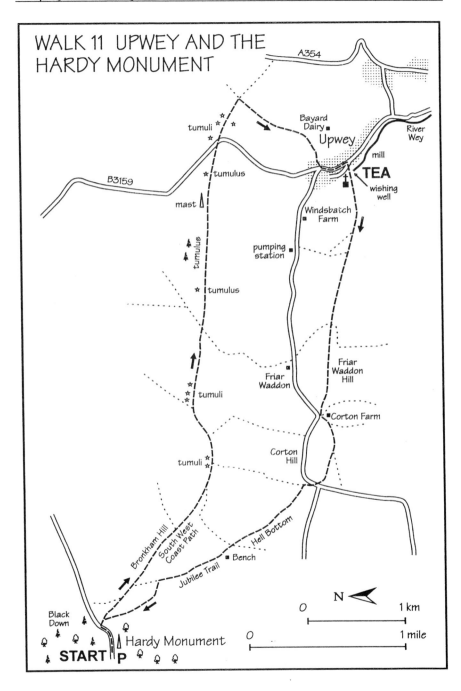

WALK 11 UPWEY AND THE HARDY MONUMENT

for a line of railway sleepers on end, many of which have waymarks. This is a permissive path, still part of the Jubilee Trail. Corton Hill is above to the right The track is just about visible as it descends to an old stile to join the public road.

Turn right and, in 70m turn left at a signposted footpath, uphill to a farm gate. Turn left to proceed along a good, wide, chalky track. In a little more than 100m go through a gate on the left and turn right to continue the same line. This route along Hell Bottom is excellent throughout, rising gently for more than 1 mile towards the Monument. The path is mainly on cropped grass, with occasional gates; the ruinous Bench Farm is passed on the way.

As the track bends a little to the right, head for a wide gap in the hedge ahead, with waymarks. Fork left here to a hedge gap on the left, where there is a bridleway waymark on a post. Go right to follow the indicated line to a waymarked gateway and continue, aiming broadly for the gap on the skyline ahead.

Go through a little gate at the top to follow a narrow path up to the public road. Turn left to return to the car park

12. Isle of Portland

Length	5½ miles
Summary	A fine, of necessity mainly coastal, walk around what most walkers will regard as the most attractive part of this highly individual area of Britain. Quite demanding for the first half mile or so, but thereafter generally easy walking.
Car Parking	Signposted free car park in a former quarry almost opposite the Portland Museum near Church Opie Cove, grid reference 697713.
Maps	Ordnance Survey Outdoor Leisure no. 15, Purbeck and South Dorset, 1:25,000 or Landranger no. 194, Dorchester and Weymouth, 1:50,000

Tea Shop

The Craft Centre and Tea Room would welcome and deserves to have more visitors. Good quality interesting crafts are for sale and the pottery is made on the premises. The small café section has appropriate seafaring decor. Everything is available from a cup of coffee to main meals and cream teas. Prices are very reasonable. Open for evening meals during high season. Unlicensed but customers are welcome to bring their own wine.

Open: all the year 10.30am – 4.30pm (minimum hours) open until 9pm in main holiday period. Closed every Monday except in high season. Tel. 01305 823611

About the Area

When viewed from the main Dorset coast, Purbeck certainly looks like an island. The low connecting causeway, which is the south east tip of Chesil Beach, is barely visible in hazy weather. Despite this connection, the peninsula does have the official title of 'Isle and Royal Manor of Portland'. It is essentially a block of solid limestone about 4 miles long and rather less than 2 miles wide. At the highest point, Verne Fort, it is 151m. (496ft.) above sea level.

For many centuries the defensive importance of this great promontory has been recognised. King Henry VIII built Portland Castle in

The museum at Portland

1539 as one of his south coast castles, on the site of a Saxon fort. Much earlier is Rufus Castle, by Church Opie Cove, traditionally ascribed to King William II (Rufus), now a gaunt ruin. In the mid 19th century, Portland Harbour was created by the laborious (23 years) construction of breakwaters to form one of the world's largest man-made harbours and an important naval base.

Extensive quarrying for several centuries has added a new dimension to the Island's natural ruggedness. The high quality of Portland stone was recognised by Sir Christopher Wren, among others, and was used in the construction of St Paul's Cathedral and many other important buildings.

At the southern tip of Portland is Portland Bill, with lighthouse, visitor centre and large car park. Villages on the Island include Fortuneswell, the largest, close to the Naval Base, Easton, Weston, and Southwell.

Visitor attractions include:

Portland Castle, adjacent to the Naval Air Station, off the Castletown road. Open daily from late March to the end of October, 10am to 6pm

St George's Church, built in 1764. Open for internal viewing during the afternoon from late May to late September.

Portland Museum, near Church Opie Cove. Housed in two thatched cottages, one of which inspired Thomas Hardy to write his novel 'The Well Beloved' around it, making the cottage the home of Avice, one of the book's heroines. Also included in the museum is a cottage occupied by Dr. Marie Stopes, the famous birth control pioneer. She was the founder and first curator of the museum in 1930; the ground floor of this cottage has been retained as a parlour, displaying her life and work. Open from Easter to October, daily other than Wednesdays and Thursdays from 10.30am to 5pm.

Tout Quarry Sculpture Park and Nature Reserve, off Wide Street, a little way south of Fortuneswell.

Broadcroft Quarry Butterfly Reserve, off Grove Road, a left turn before reaching Easton village centre when driving from Weymouth.

Although it is assumed that tea shop walkers will normally use motor vehicles to and from their chosen destinations, it is worth mentioning that there is a frequent service of buses, some of them open topped in summer, from K5 bus stop by the King's Statue on Weymouth Esplanade.

The Walk

From the car park cross the road and turn left towards the Portland Museum. Proceed along the surfaced roadway, signposted as 'public footpath', towards Church Opie Cove, soon passing under an arch, part of the ruin of Rufus Castle, then turning right to descend a great flight of steps – 153 in all. Part way down belvedere with seats is a good viewpoint.

Continue the descent past masses of red valerian to a signposted diversion to the right. This leads to the ruins of the 13th century church of St Andrew and its graveyard, where there are at least two tombstones carved with the skull and crossbones. Go down to Church Opie Cove, a pleasant place but rather over endowed with beach huts of variable quality. There are basic public conveniences.

Leave the cove by a track rising up steps behind the beach huts. For about half a mile this track winds in and out and up and down, dividing and re-uniting as it passes through the area of the Southwell Landslip, adorned with valerian and many other colourful plants, an attractive but quite demanding section of the walk. Reach Cheyne Weares, a scenic car parking area and turn inland for a few metres to the road. Turn left to walk along the roadside verge for about a quarter of a mile to a 'public footpath' signpost.

Turn left here along an excellent stony track angling towards the sea. Obviously a former quarry roadway, this track makes a fine coastal walking route. Follow a 'coast path' marker stone at a junction to continue past old quarries and more old quarries, always close to the sea, with wonderfully colourful banks of thrift along the way.

Go over a waymarked footbridge as the Bill is approached and pass numerous and varied beach huts, a real shanty town described as 'lawnsheds' by the Ordnance Survey, to reach the end of the road, the lighthouse, the public conveniences and various catering premises – a kind of second division Land's End.

Walk round the back of the lighthouse to commence the return. Pass a 'coast path' marker stone and the public conveniences, then keep to the right of a Ministry of Defence establishment on a defined path over grass. Although not quite the right of way shown on Ordnance Survey, this inviting path is obviously well-used as it angles towards the sea, continuing to rise along the top of the cliffs towards the Portland coastguard lookout station, where the tracks come together.

The way is now straightforward as it passes the large and rather desolate Southwell Business Park. The Weston residential area looms ahead and the sea is visible to east and west. After the business park there are four junctions with right turns; it is approximately half a mile to the fourth of these, well before the built-up area.

Turn right here, at an 'East Cliffs' marker stone. A good wide path leads, with left then right kinks, to a main north/south road, Weston Road. Cross over into Weston Street. In about 100m the tea shop/craft centre is on the right.

Continue along Weston Street, where there is a grass verge until, 100m short of the junction with a main road, turn left on to a signposted stony track between a quarry and its works buildings, fenced on both sides. Turn right at the quarry exit roadway, walk for a few metres to the main road, and turn left to return to the car park.

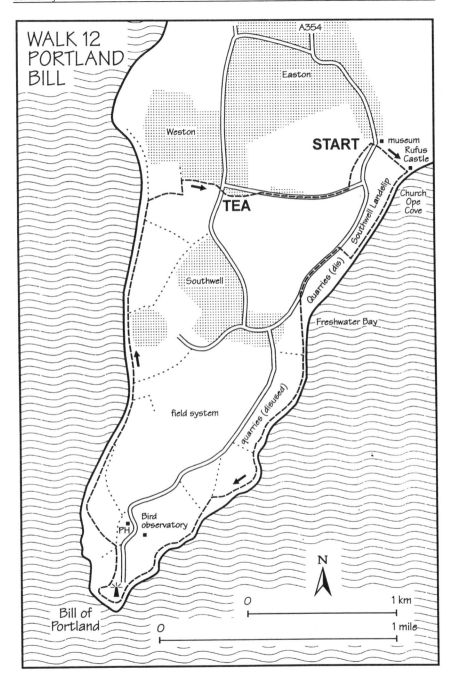

WALK 12
PORTLAND
BILL

A354

Easton

Weston

START · museum
Rufus
Castle ■

Southwell Landslip

TEA

Church
Ope
Cove

Quarries (dis)

Southwell

Freshwater Bay

field system

quarries (disused)

Bird
observatory
PH ■

N

0   1 km

Bill of
Portland   0   1 mile

13. Ringstead and Osmington Mills

Length	4¾ miles
Summary	An excellent circular walk on good tracks along high downland, then down to the sea and along the South West Coast Path to Ringstead and Osmington Mills. The inland return is also attractive with only the crossing of one large field and a steep little climb as possibly onerous.
Car Parking	National Trust free car parking area on high ground accessed from the cul de sac road to Ringstead, signposted from the A353 main road between Osmington and Poxwell, grid reference 757824.
Maps	Ordnance Survey Outdoor Leisure no. 15, Purbeck and South Dorset, 1:25,000 or Landranger no. 194, Dorchester and Weymouth, 1:50,000.

Tea Shop

The Cottage Tea Room is a little café in a beautiful scenic location. It is not easy to describe this refreshment facility. It is certainly popular for the purchase of ice cream and there is seating in the garden for those wishing to have tea, coffee, or cold drinks; limited choice of sandwiches, and cakes. In the conservatory building, there are some tables for cooler days. Second-hand books are also sold here.

Open: times are somewhat unstructured. Open in winter if weather is suitable but equally may be closed from time to time in the summer.

Alternative venues: Ringstead Bay Beach café – definitely summer months and only outdoor seating. The Smugglers Inn at Osmington Mills (very near to The Cottage Tea Room) offers the usual range of inn food. It has a large attractive outdoor terrace.

About the Area

Although quite close to the Weymouth built-up area, the coast around Ringstead and Osmington Mills is prime Dorset. Both are small settlements, that at Osmington Mills straggling inland along a shallow valley from the beautifully situated Smugglers Inn.

Built earlier this century by a local family, the Chapel of St

Smugglers Inn, Osmington Mills

Catherine by the Sea, near Ringstead, is remarkable. About the size of a large garden shed and of not dissimilar structure, the chapel has a wonderful sea-facing site with a prominent rustic cross. It remains consecrated.

The Walk

Walk along the car park roadway, away from the surfaced road, to a gate/stile. Continue along this track, with good views behind to Portland and the town of Weymouth. Before reaching the isolated building of Sea Barn Farm, turn right at the second of two adjacent tracks, close to a National Trust 'Ringstead Bay' sign. This is another good track; bear right at a fork with a stone marker 'Ringstead 1', joining the South West Coast Path and descending down a tarmac road. Look out for St Catherine's by the Sea Chapel on the left, an unpretentious wooden hut, with information board inside.

On approaching a thatched house, bear left to the corner of a grassy area and continue along the obvious path by a 'Ringstead ½' marker stone. Cross two tiny streams on footbridges as the path passes through a densely shrubby area. Pass Creek static caravan site to reach Ringstead, with large car park, public conveniences and a comprehensive beach shop with some refreshments.

Turn towards the sea; the marker stone has 'Osmington 1¾ miles', something of an exaggeration; go ahead through a gate to pass in front of a few houses. Opposite the last house fork left at a 'coast path' marker and 'Osmington 1' sign (more accurate) and go over a footbridge. For some distance the path is narrow and part overgrown.

Descend a few steps to a stream with bridge and yet another marker stone. Rise over a minor headland. Behind, the headland of White Nothe, beyond Ringstead, is impressive. Ahead, the Osmington Mills area is now in view. Descend to the rear of the Smugglers Inn. Rise to the road and turn left to the tea shop, beautifully situated on a little promontory.

After tea, walk up the road, passing the public conveniences; 20 metres after the telephone box turn right at an 'Osmington Round Walk' sign to descend the bank on a narrow path. Cross a footbridge and go up steps and then to the left across the backs of a row of dwellings, to a waymarked stile. Turn left a few metres after the stile to rise across a field on a well-used path. Go over a waymarked stile and pass Kingfisher Glades pine lodges. At a surfaced lane turn right.

At a junction by a bungalow follow 'Spring Bottom ¼', passing the bungalow and another house, to a stile on the left. From here the car park can be seen. A clear track descends to Spring Bottom, fording a shallow stream. Go straight ahead through a gate/stile into woodland with a 'Ringstead 1¼' signpost. Keep straight on at a signposted junction, go left at a junction by a bungalow, and join the Ringstead access road.

Turn right to stride along the road for less than a quarter of a mile and then, as the road bends to the right, turn left over a waymarked stile. Continue over another stile on the far side of a narrow field. Cross a stream on a footbridge and head straight across a large rising field, nearly a quarter of a mile in distance. The route is barely worn, but ease or otherwise of progress will depend very much on the length of the grass at the particular time.

Reach a broad, stony, access track at a gate/stile and signpost, near South Down Farm. Turn left, pass the farm, with its handsome Georgian farmhouse, and tackle the steepest part of the return to the car park on the surfaced farm road, passing a chalk pit on the right. The road reaches the top of the down by the car park entrance.

WALK 13 RINGSTEAD AND OSMINGTON MILLS

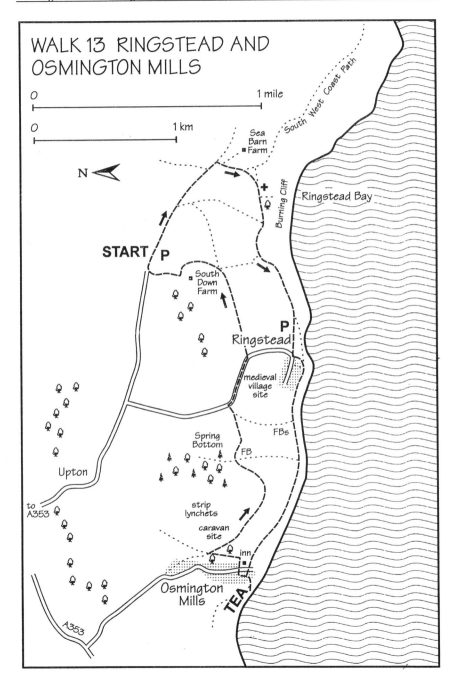

0 ————————————————————— 1 mile

0 ————————————————————— 1 km

South West Coast Path

N

Sea Barn Farm

Burning Cliff

Ringstead Bay

START P

South Down Farm

P

Ringstead

medieval village site

FBs

Spring Bottom

FB

Upton

strip lynchets

caravan site

inn

to A353

Osmington Mills

TEA

A353

14. Lulworth Cove and Durdle Door

Length	3 miles
Summary	A superb little walk linking two of the great features of the Dorset coast. Entirely straightforward and, apart from some mud, very good paths. Climbs to 125m. (410ft.) but at reasonable gradients.
Car Parking	Car park above Durdle Door, with access past the caravan site. Leave the public road less than one mile west of West Lulworth village, at Newlands Farm. Grid reference 811805.
Maps	Ordnance Survey Outdoor Leisure no. 15, Purbeck and South Dorset, 1:25,000 or Landranger no. 194, Dorchester and Weymouth, 1:50,000.

Tea Shop

The unpretentious café at the cove is literally at the water edge – stunning views – spectacular situation. On a good sunny day it is heavenly to enjoy food and drink sitting on the beach amidst the bustle of boats. Refreshments available here range from burger and chips, sandwiches, tea, coffee, to ice cream. The board outside promises "service with a smile"!
Open: 10am – 5.30pm. Tel. 01929 400648.

About the Area

Lulworth Cove must be the outstanding feature of the Dorset coast. Almost circular, like a mountain tarn with steep plunging cliffs but with an outlet to the sea, this wonder of nature never fails to attract. The cliffs themselves, where the Cove bites hard into the western end of Bindon Hill, are of great geological interest, with highly visible folds in the colourful rock – the 'Lulworth Crumple'.

From the nearby village of West Lulworth, with its heritage centre and large car park, a narrow cul de sac road leads purposefully to the tiny shingle beach and the tea shop.Durdle Door, a natural archway, is an intriguing example of the power of the sea in wearing down the coastal Portland stone. To the east of the Cove, not on the line of this

Beach café, Lulworth Cove

walk, the 'Fossil Forest' is an area with the fossilised remains of a great prehistoric forest.

More than two miles inland from West Lulworth, along the road towards Wareham, the smaller village of East Lulworth has the restored 17th century Lulworth Castle, open to the public throughout the year. For further details and opening hours, telephone 01929 400352.

The Walk

Leave the car park at a gate along a broad track heading downhill towards the sea. In about 40m turn right, opposite a double stile. The track is now barely marked on the grass, but stay roughly parallel with the fence which marks the boundary of the caravan site.

Rise slightly; the track now becomes clearer as it descends to a stile to head for the valley known, believe it or not, as Scratchy Bottom. Before the valley bear left, to go down steeply towards the sea Go over a stile and join the South West Coast Path. Durdle Door is

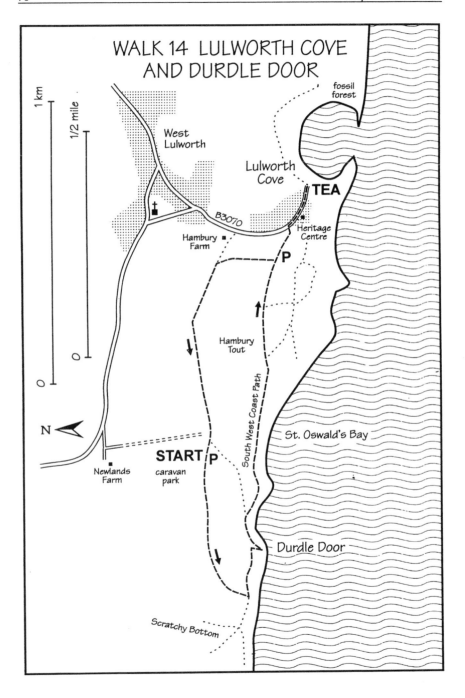

WALK 14 LULWORTH COVE
AND DURDLE DOOR

visible; turn left to walk to the main viewing area, where there are steps down to the beach.

Continue towards Lulworth Cove and follow what is probably the most used section of the whole coast path – a quarter of a million walkers per annum – making sure to keep right at a fork before passing close to the top of Hambury Tout and starting the long descent directly to the car park at the Lulworth Heritage Centre. Needless to say, the coastal views are superb.

Turn right, downhill, along the cul de sac road to the Cove, where the Beach Café has a wonderful waterside situation.

Return to the Heritage Centre car park and to the start of the coast path, but turn right immediately after a stile. There is a stone sign 'Durdle Door avoiding steep and loose section of coast path'. This minor path now follows the line of a fence, curving to the left above Hambury Farm. In this area the path might be muddy after rain but, after a stile, conditions underfoot improve as the route rises steadily along the bottom edge of fields, with stiles at the boundaries, before returning directly to the car park.

```
┌─────────────────────────────────────────────────────────────┐
│                                                               │
│                  15. Kimmeridge                               │
│                                                               │
└─────────────────────────────────────────────────────────────┘
```

Length	3 miles
Summary	Another short but quite varied walk, with a tiny section of the South West Coast Path, some high downland, and a length of the Smedmore Estate coastal road. Apart from one very short steep descent, entirely easy underfoot. The rise from the sea to Kimmeridge village is very steady, followed by a short, sharp, rise up to the car park.
Car Parking	Free parking in a disused quarry above Kimmeridge village, grid reference 919800. Information boards but no public conveniences until Kimmeridge Bay.
Maps	Ordnance Survey Outdoor Leisure no. 15, Purbeck and South Dorset, 1:25,000 or Landranger no.195, Bournemouth and Purbeck, 1:50,000.

Tea Shop

Seven Taps Café is part of the post office in Kimmeridge. The thatched building is wonderfully situated in this hamlet close to the sea. There are plenty of walkers in the area, especially at weekends and all are welcome at this café. Everything is served here from ice creams to plaice and chips. Outdoor seating for sunny days.
Open: 9am -5.30pm every day all year and until 7.30pm in main season but will close earlier in the winter months. Tel. 01929 480701.

About the Area

This walk is based on Kimmeridge, a stone and thatch village cradled by a great sweep of high downland. Quiet except in high season, Kimmeridge has just the general store/tea shop and a street which descends along a shallow valley towards the sea. The restored church, which looks down the street, has only a doorway as evidence of its Norman origins.

To the south-east is Smedmore House, not normally open to the public, a 17th century building in a large expanse of parkland. Much of the land in the Kimmeridge area is part of the Smedmore Estate.

On the beach is a Marine Reserve Centre operated by the Dorset

The tea shop at Kimmeridge

Wildlife Trust. To the west of Kimmeridge are extensive army training areas, with public access only when permitted by the Ministry of
Defence. The oil-bearing shale of the Kimmeridge Bay cliffs has had
a small on-shore oil rig for many years.

Prominent on a cliff top close to the sea is Clavel's Tower, a folly
built in 1831. The Clavel family have long been associated with the
Smedmore Estate.

The Walk

From the old quarry car park turn right, uphill, along the road for
50m, then turn left at the second of two adjacent signposts, at a
gate/stile with 'Range Walks' waymarking. For about half a mile the
well-used track goes along the edge of a cultivated field and the top
of the scarp, with great views to sea and over the rooftops of
Kimmeridge.

Turn sharp left over a waymarked stile at a stone marker
'Kimmeridge church ¾, Bay ¾', to follow part of the Hardy Way angling down the side of the scarp on a minor but clear path among

gorse. After about 150m turn right at a marker stone for a short, steep descent to a marker post at the foot and an obvious track across fields, aiming straight for the prominent Clavel tower on its headland.

The path goes straight on, gently downhill, towards Kimmeridge Bay, passing the occasional waymarked gate and stile. The oil rig can be seen to the right. Join a surfaced road, pass public conveniences (there are better ones a little further), turn left and then right along a broad, stony, track which is part of a (rather expensive) car parking area.

Keep close to the edge, above the sea. passing information boards, and take the path leaving the car park at the far end. Turn right at a signpost 'Quay and information centre' to go down a few steps, cross a stream on a footbridge and reach the quay area. Here is the Purbeck Marine Wildlife Reserve with the Dorset Wildlife Trust Centre and a seat to enjoy views of Kimmeridge Bay.

Go left up to the Smedmore Estate toll road and follow this road uphill, shortly passing better public conveniences, all the way back to Kimmeridge village. The tea shop is unmissable in this small village.

To return to the car park, continue up the road and go straight ahead up steps to St Nicholas Church. Pass along the edge of the churchyard and through an old kissing gate to tackle the scarp. The grass is just about worn on this short sharp rise, which joins the public road at a stile. Turn right for a few metres to return to the old quarry.

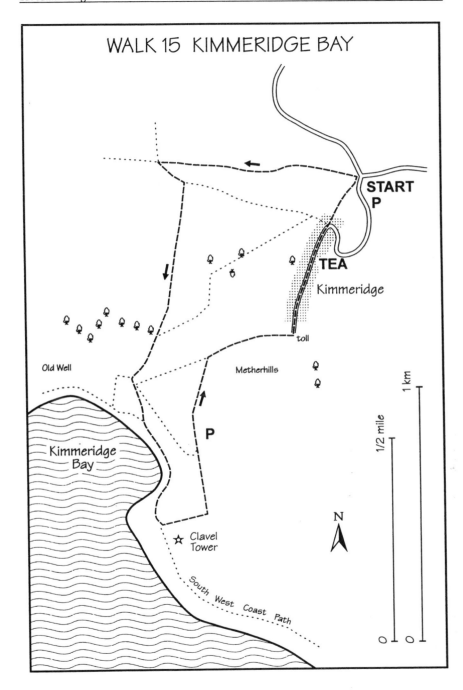

WALK 15 KIMMERIDGE BAY

START
P

TEA

Kimmeridge

toll

Old Well

Metherhills

P

Kimmeridge
Bay

Clavel
Tower

South West Coast Path

N

1/2 mile

1 km

16. Worth Matravers and St Aldhelm's head

Length	4 ¼ miles (full circuit)
Summary	Basically a circuit of St Aldhelm's Head, using a good length of the South West Coast Path, with a visit to the nearby village of Worth Matravers and to the old chapel on the headland. Nice, easy, walking, always good underfoot, but with a significant fall and rise at the mouth of a combe.
Car Parking	Roughish free car park by Renscombe Farm, accessed by a cul de sac road to the west from Worth Matravers village, grid reference 964775.
Maps	Ordnance Survey Outdoor Leisure no. 15, Purbeck and South Dorset, 1:25,000 or Landranger no. 195, Bournemouth and Purbeck, 1:50,000

Tea Shop

The Craft Centre and Café is just a short distance from the tiny village centre. The café is mixed in with the crafts in this old farm building. Historical photographs of ship wrecks and local scenes are round the walls and the room is open to the underside of the old stone roof. The tiled floor is "boot friendly"; the stove is lit on cool days whilst for sunny days there is seating outdoors. At the time of our visit there was some impressive pottery for sale as well as other well made craft items – a good opportunity to resolve "don't know what to buy" presents. In the café area cooked meals start with breakfast available until 11am. Lunches include "Ploughman's" with Dorset Blue Vinny or "Fisherman's" with smoked mackerel – both served with granary bread. There are also omelettes and jacket potatoes; listed on the blackboard are cooked platters of the day. Cream teas, all kinds of cakes, coffee or tea served in mugs or cups, are always available.

Open: Every day except Tuesdays from 9.15am – 5pm. If visiting out of season it may be a good idea to telephone to check opening hours. Tel. 01929 439360.

About the Area

St Aldhelm's Head juts out boldly into the English Channel, with the South West Coast Path following faithfully round the top of the cliffs. This provides a wonderful opportunity for a circuit which is two thirds by the coast. At the hub is Worth Matravers, a lovely village built in the Purbeck stone which is still extensively quarried in the vicinity. The church has a Norman tower, an exceptionally good Norman chancel arch and much more of interest. In the churchyard is buried a local farmer by the name of Benjamin Jesty who, having noted the association of cowpox with the absence of smallpox, successfully experimented in 1774 with primitive inoculation on his wife and two sons. This was some years before the more widely known and acclaimed success of Jenner in this field.

The tiny Norman chapel dedicated to St Aldhelm stands alone on the windswept headland. The square shape and the orientation are both very unusual. Believed to be originally built as a chantry, its history is more of legend than of fact, but there is a first mention in the reign of King Henry III (1216-1272). The chapel was falling into disrepair in the 17th century, ruinous by the 18th and restored for

Worth Matravers

worship in the 19th. Used rather spasmodically during the earlier part of the present century, more restoration during the last 30 years has led to regular use.

Stone, the so-called 'Purbeck marble' has been quarried at least since Roman times; in the middle ages it was used in the construction of Westminster Abbey and Salisbury Cathedral. Although the activity is widespread in the Worth Matravers area, there is less damage to the landscape than might be expected. The last operational sea cliff quarry, closed in the 1950s, was at West Winspit, where the extensive underground workings are still very evident, although the site is regarded as potentially dangerous and there is no public right of entrance. Flat bottomed boats were used to carry the stone from the quarry.

The Walk

Leave the car park by the stile at the far end to bear right along a broad level track across cultivated fields, towards the sea, with an intermediate gate/stile. At a second gate/stile, join the South West Coast Path, turning left.

Below is Chapman's Pool, with Egmont Point opposite. The walking is virtually level, on pleasant grass high above the sea. Pass the Royal Marines (Dorset) Memorial, set in a well-kept tiny garden.

Descend a long flight of steps, cross the mouth of an apparently unnamed combe, and then ascend even more steps. If at the bottom of this combe you can't face the ascent, there is a right of way to the left, along the combe bottom, back towards the car park. From the top of the steps it is only a few strides to two unusual memorial seats and then the coastguard station and, more interestingly, the chapel of St Aldhelm, obviously kept in good repair. *By turning inland here, there is another opportunity to short cut the walk.*

Continue along the S.W.C.P., descending to the right to avoid a 'no right of way' field. The path is now not so high above the sea and there is a good array of flowers, including the lovely thrift by the wayside. At the foot of the next combe is Winspit, with its most impressive former sea quarry. Interestingly, there is evidence of the use of bricks in the construction of some quarry buildings.

Turn left to take a good path rising gently up the combe, with plenty of gorse initially. Worth Matravers is soon in view. As the road forks keep right at a marker stone 'Worth ½'. Go over a stile and

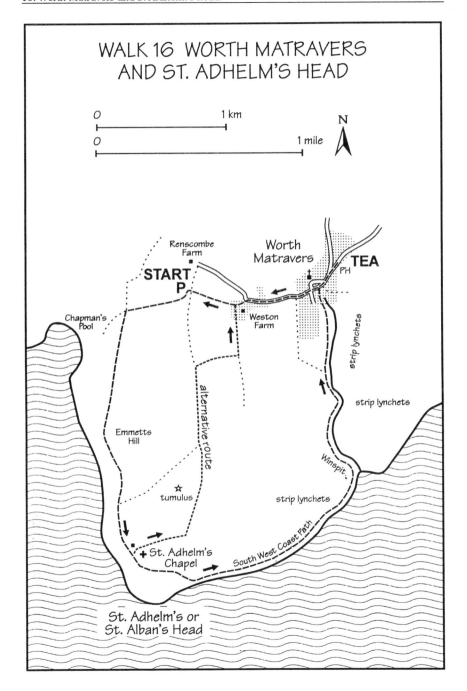

WALK 16 WORTH MATRAVERS AND ST. ADHELM'S HEAD

rise more steeply across a little meadow. Two more stiles (one double) lead directly into the village. Turn right for a short distance and keep right to reach the craft centre/tea shop.

Return to the village centre and walk along the car park access road as far as Weston Farm. Turn left here at a 'St Aldhelm's Head' signpost, then right in 70m at a 'Chapman's Pool 1' signpost. A well-defined path by a fence leads directly back to the car park.

---

17. Corfe Castle

Length	6 ¼ miles
Summary	Generally an easy, fairly level walk, around some of the lovely Purbeck countryside. Paths generally good, with some mud in wet weather. The walk is based on Corfe Castle, one of the finest villages in Dorset.
Car Parking	At Norden 'Park and Ride' at the terminus of the preserved railway line, well signposted at the roundabout on A351. Donations requested Grid reference, 957829. Alternatively, there is a public car park by the side of the A351 a quarter of a mile north of Corfe Castle village.
Maps	Ordnance Survey Outdoor Leisure no. 15, Purbeck and South Dorset 1:25,000 or Landranger no. 195, Bournemouth and Purbeck 1:50,000

Tea Shop

The National Trust Tea Shop by the castle entrance is almost the first building as one approaches the village following a longish walk – a welcome sight indeed. Decor here is plain and appropriate – wooden floors and furniture. The atmosphere is bustling and the service cheerful.

Good selection of food including some hot dishes (traditional roast on Sundays at lunch time), cream teas of course, and home made cakes but beware! portions of the large cakes are enormous!

Open: Easter/April 1st to end of October 10am – 5.30pm daily. November to March closes at 4.30pm. Also closed for a period in Jan/Feb for redecoration – if in doubt, telephone first. Tel. 01929 481332.

About the Area

From whichever direction one approaches the village, the gaunt ruins of Corfe Castle dominate, the shattered walls and dismantled turrets still rising defiantly more than 300 years after Cromwell's men struggled to blow it up. What a stronghold this must have been, controlling the only significant route through the long ridge of the Purbeck Hills.

As might be expected, the castle has a long and complex history. Although the date of construction is not known, its first recorded siege was during the brief reign of King Stephen. At the time of King John it was used as a royal prison and for the disposal of many of that brutal King's perceived enemies. The castle's final period of use was during the Civil War, when internal betrayal led to its capture by Parliamentary forces in 1646. Now cared for by the National Trust, it is open to the public from 10am to 5pm March to October and from 11am to 3.30pm in winter.

At the foot of the castle mound a fine village has developed over the centuries, with inns and shops adding to the attraction of the stone cottages. Although the position at the heart of the Isle of Purbeck ensures the popularity of Corfe, the village has, on the whole, been kept remarkably free of the worst excesses of tourism. There is small museum in West Street.

The present Swanage Railway uses part of the track-bed of the former Wareham to Swanage branch line of the Southern Railway. At present services, mostly steam-powered, operate between Swanage and the park and ride at Norden, a little way beyond Corfe Castle, the principal intermediate station. There is some activity for most of the

Swanage railway at Corfe Castle

year, excluding January to March (unless Easter falls in the latter month) and there are special operations such as Santa Specials and dining excursions. It is intended to extend the line as far as the original junction at Wareham.

The 'Blue Pool' is a local beauty spot, a Site of Special Scientific Interest, with visitor facilities including refreshments and a children's play area. It is open to the public (on payment), from March to November in respect of the gardens and from Easter to early October for the facilities.

The Walk

Leave the car park by a kissing gate at the far end and turn left towards 'Scotland ½'. Cross a road to a flight of steps and a waymarked stile. Follow a narrow track worn across a field, to woodland, entered by another waymarked stile. The track through the trees, mainly silver birch, is always clear on the ground, weaving a little but keeping roughly parallel with the right-hand boundary fence.

Keep right at an apparent fork. After an old gate and two more stiles, cross a large cultivated field; the right of way bears slightly to the right. Keep to the right-hand boundary where there is attractive light woodland. Exit at a waymarked stile into rough woodland, keep right at a fork. The path now winds through gorse, then heather and a boardwalk over a swamp as Scotland Farm is approached.

Reach a minor road and an informative National Trust board concerning Hartland Moor. Turn left along the very minor road, with bramble-clad verges. The ruins of Corfe Castle are silhouetted against the sky. In less than quarter of a mile fork right, over a cattle grid, into a farm trackway with a bridleway waymark, soon reaching New Line Farm.

Bear left by a waymarked post along a concrete roadway and then right to pass the farm buildings. Continue along the access road to reach the main Wareham to Corfe Castle road. Cross diagonally left by a cottage dated 1710, with a certificated caravan site. After passing a duck pond turn left over a waymarked stile and follow yellow arrows indicating a winding route, partly in woodland, to avoid private property on the right.

Pass a second entrance to the private area, cross an entrance drive, and bear right to continue through woodland. Leave the woodland at a defunct gate, cross a plank bridge, and rise across a wet area; at really wet times the path also does duty as a stream. At the kissing gate at the top, there are several footpath signs including a modern stone. Keep right to head for 'Furzebrook 1'. To shorten the walk you can turn left here for 'East Creech'.

The path has yellow waymarks as it crosses the heath, rich in heather and dwarf gorse, with just a few small trees. There are more waymarks on posts as a wider track is joined, close to a fence, the boundary of the Blue Pool land. Keep right, to a gate, go through a kissing gate and enter woodland, largely coniferous. Join a major path, keeping left to reach the entrance to the Blue Pool. Opposite is a large car park/picnic area.

Visit or pass by the Blue Pool, bearing left to a no exit – one way traffic sign. Go along the surfaced access road, soon reaching a minor public road. Turn left for 200m and then, as the road bends to the right, take a waymarked path on the left, well used through light woodland. Pass a specialised nature reserve and continue along this delightful path until it rises to a gate and on to the minor road.

Ten metres before the road turn left on the 'Purbeck Way', with other waymarks including 'Corfe'. At a pond turn right over a footbridge, then left, with 'Corfe' and 'Norden Farm' signposted. The ridge of the Purbeck Hills is now fairly close on the right. At a signposted junction turn right to 'Corfe 1½', go over a stile and along the edge of a field, over more stiles, rising across a small meadow.

At the top stile turn left to take the lower of two paths contouring along the hillside partly among trees. The fine views include Wareham. After a view of Corfe Castle bear left, go over a stile, and descend to a junction with two stiles. Turn right here to continue to a minor road. Turn left for about 50m, cross a bridge, and turn right towards 'castle entrance', soon reaching the village, with the tea shop immediately on the left.

After refreshments walk up the castle entrance and turn right through a gate to follow a little track with an N.T. waymark across the side of the castle mound. Descend to a gate and cross the main road to a car park. Go through the car park to a flight of steps up the bank at the back. Bear left by the railway line, cross stiles and turn right, over the line, then left at a 'park and ride ¾, Scotland 1¼' sign to take a well-used path along the edge of a field and into woodland at another stile.

At the next junction either 'park and ride/Scotland' or 'Norden platform' will provide a return direct to the car park.

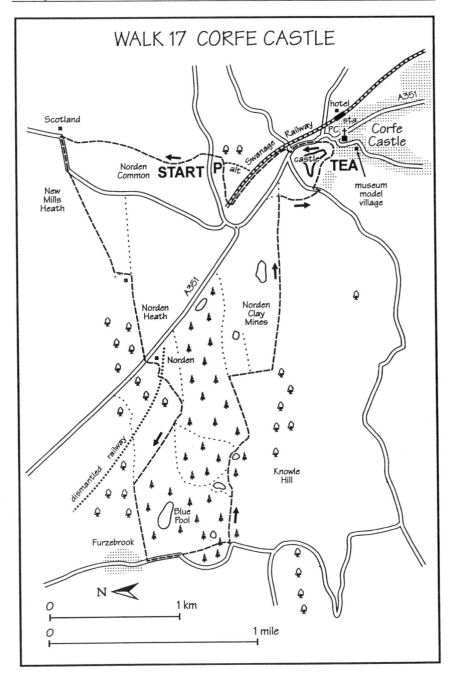

WALK 17 CORFE CASTLE

```
┌─────────────────────────────────────────────────────────────────┐
│                                                                   │
│  ┌─────────────────────────────────────────────────────────────┐ │
│  │                                                             │ │
│  │       18. Studland and Ballard Down                         │ │
│  │                                                             │ │
│  └─────────────────────────────────────────────────────────────┘ │
│                                                                   │
└─────────────────────────────────────────────────────────────────┘
```

Length	4 miles
Summary	A very fine walk indeed including the ascent of Ballard Down, a section along the top of the downland with wonderful views over two bays, and a section of the South West Coast Path returning to Studland, passing the Old Harry Rocks on the way. All the ascent, a total of about 100m (328ft.), occurs early in the walk and is not excessively steep. The paths are superb throughout and the need for navigation is minimal.
Car Parking	National Trust car park serving the south beach at Studland village, grid reference 037825. There are public conveniences a few metres along the road.
Maps	Ordnance Survey Outdoor Leisure no. 15, Purbeck and South Dorset, 1:25,000 or Landranger no. 195, Bournemouth and Purbeck, 1:50,000.

Tea Shop

It was only at our third attempt that we found the tea room at Manor Farm open but it was worth waiting for. The café, housed in a farm building, is spacious and well furnished with dark wood tables and chairs. There is also outdoor seating mixed in with a collection of preserved old agricultural machinery. Light lunches here include home-made soup and crusty bread, quiche and salad, toasted sandwiches, etc. Later in the day one may prefer a cream tea and choose from jam sponge, chocolate or fruit cakes. There is an impressive array of food hygiene certificates and welcome host awards displayed on the dresser.

Open: 11.30am – 5pm from Easter to end of September everyday but beware that hours can be temperamental outside peak periods, so it may be preferable to telephone if in doubt. Tel. 01929 450538.

About the Area

At the eastern end of the distinctive Isle of Purbeck part of Dorset, the long spine of the Purbeck Hills reaches the sea, ending abruptly at The Foreland or Handfast Point, with magnificent white cliffs.

Several of the great detached rocks have quaint names such as 'Old Harry' and 'Old Harry's Wife'.

To the south of this spine of downland is the long established seaside holiday town of Swanage, despite its various attractions still comparatively quiet and traditional. For details of the Swanage Railway see walk no. 17.

Studland: Manor Farm

To the north is the scattered village of Studland at the near end of several miles of sandy beach extending all the way to the car ferry which plies across the mouth of Poole Harbour. Included are a nature reserve and a legitimate naturist beach. The reserve and the beaches are owned by the National Trust, with a visitor centre at Knoll Beach. The old part of Studland village is grouped along several little lanes off the rather less attractive main road, with the parish church of St Nicholas, the old Manor Farm and some stone cottages. The church is almost entirely Norman, although several windows have been modified.

The Walk

Leave the car park by the stile at the lower end, crossing a small meadow behind the Bankes Arms Hotel, then joining a road over another stile. Turn right. In a short distance, as the road bends, there is a carved cross dated 1976.

Turn left here at Manor Farm, noting the tea room for future reference. There is a 'Ballard Down. Swanage' signpost. Follow a surfaced lane, soon rising gently towards the modern Glebelands Estate. In these times of comprehensive town and country planning controls the construction of this estate does seem to be somewhat questionable in an attractive rural area.

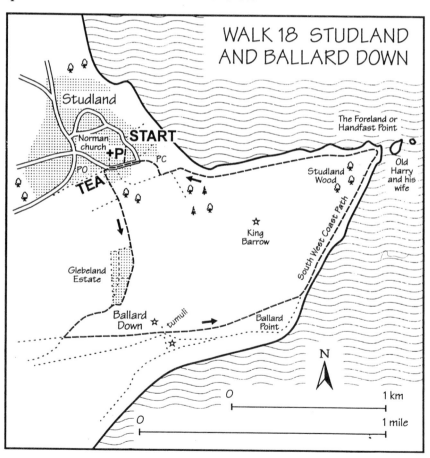

WALK 18 STUDLAND AND BALLARD DOWN

Go straight on at a junction and bear right at the top of the estate. Go through a gate on the left, signposted 'Swanage 1½' and enter the National Trust Ballard Down Estate. A fine track rises diagonally across the hillside, the effort of ascent being rewarded by the views of Studland Bay, Poole Harbour and Brownsea Island. The best reward of all is to reach the ridge, with a post, a marker stone and a stone bench dated 1852, with a 'rest and be thankful' inscription. At this point Swanage Bay comes into view.

Turn left to follow a delightful wide path along the crest of the Down for the best part of one mile. Towards the far end is a trig. point, followed by a gentle descent above Ballard Point. The South West Coast path joins us, almost unnoticed, on the right. Continue to the sharp point of The Foreland/Handfast Point, highlighted by the brilliant white of Old Harry and his fellows. The wayside is brightened by bluebells, red campion and cowslips in Spring. The perspicacious will already have noticed that this scene constitutes the front cover illustration of O.S. Outdoor Leisure Map no. 15.

Hang on to young children here! Turn left for the last mile back to Studland, initially along the northern edge of Studland Wood, which has an organised woodland walk. As throughout this walk, the track is always entirely clear. Reach a road beside public conveniences and turn left to go to Manor Farm in less than 200m.

Return to the car park either wholly along the road or by using the initial short length of path behind the Bankes Arms.

19. Brownsea Island

Length	2½ miles (variable)
Summary	Truly a walk with a difference. Few walking guides, with or without associated tea shops, can offer a choice which includes this fine island. Entirely easy walking on broad tracks for which, I am bound to whisper, boots are not really necessary. The highest part of Brownsea is only 24m. (80ft.) above sea level, but the landscape is more diverse than might be expected. Note that dogs are not allowed on the island. Inevitably there are ferry costs, and also landing fees for those who are not members of the National Trust, but the island does offer a great deal which will be of interest, such as fun trails for children and a substantial nature reserve; the little journey on the boat is always enjoyable.
Car Parking	National Trust car park (in season, non members of the National Trust may have to pay) close to the tip of the peninsula north of Studland, grid reference 036865. Note; there is some roadside parking nearby.
Maps	Ordnance Survey Outdoor Leisure no. 15, Purbeck and South Dorset, 1:25,000 or Landranger no. 195, Bournemouth and Purbeck, 1:50,000 On the island the National Trust has free leaflets with larger scale plans.

Tea Shop

After landing and a few minutes spent browsing at the information point, we welcomed a cup of coffee sitting in the court yard before starting the walk to explore Brownsea Island. Returning to the quay a few hours later we were ready to do justice to lunch in the National Trust owned café. The range of food is offered all day – from cooked meals to cold drinks there is plenty of choice. It is counter service in this light, bright café overlooking Poole Harbour and depending on the weather one may opt for indoors or for the sheltered court yard setting – either provides a peaceful experience.

Open: 10.30am to 30 minutes before the last boat departs – from Easter/April to early October. Tel. 01202 700244.

About the Area

An island sitting in the middle of Poole Harbour might not be immediately obvious as the site of a prospective Tea Shop Walk. It does,
however, work very well. Apart from this excellent little walk, there
is a substantial nature reserve, managed by the Dorset Wildlife
Trust, with limited public access. Over the whole island there is interesting wildlife, including the rare and threatened native red
squirrel. Much of Brownsea is wooded, with a good variety of trees.

Ask the average person what he or she knows about Brownsea Island, and the answer is likely to be 'boy scout camps'. Used from
1907 by Baden-Powell, founder of the scout movement, part of the
island became the most famous of all camp sites. This use continues
and there are two monuments to Baden-Powell himself.

Less well-known is Brownsea's industrial history, largely brick
and tile making close to the southern and western shores. Although
brick making using the suitable local clay started earlier, it was in
the mid 19th century that Col. Waugh developed and extended the
industry. One works had seven kilns and a building no less than
90m long, 30m wide, and three floors in height. Products included

Ferry boats at Sandbanks

sanitary ware such as drain pipes, very evident from the crushed fragments on much of the path nearby. Another works not far away was linked to the 'New Pier' of 1855 by a railway line. This pier is still evident. In 1855 the Colonel also built a little village to house the pottery workers, naming it Maryland after his wife. Damaged by German bombers in World War II, the village was finally demolished in 1961. Just a few traces remain on the ground.

The island church of St Mary the Virgin was also built for Col. Waugh, in 1854. At the base of the tower is a superior area, with fireplace, reserved for the Colonel and his family.

Brownsea Castle dates from 1547, its gun batteries defending Poole Harbour. It was later converted to a stately home and there are 18th and 19th century additions. Over the years there has been associated farming, an extensive kitchen garden and a vinery with a large surviving brick wall. Heated pipes here enabled the growth of grapes, peaches and figs.

The Walk

From the recommended car park walk for about 200m to the Studland to Sandbanks motor car ferry (the modest foot passenger fare is paid on the return journey. The ferry operates at 20 minute intervals until 11pm). At Sandbanks turn left to the booking kiosk and quay of Brownsea Island Ferries Ltd. for the shortest crossing to the island. The frequency is half hourly in high season, hourly in low season (tel. 01202 666226 or 01929 462383 if in doubt)

Land at the National Trust quay and pass through the information centre building, obtaining any necessary leaflets. Bear left to follow a signpost 'church and south shore'. Brownsea Castle is to the left. Pass a little bust of Baden-Powell, then a nature reserve hide. Continue along the broad, easy, track, turning left at a 'south shore' signpost.

Pass St Mary's Church and an area with many peacocks and some unusual poultry. As the track forks bear right towards 'Scout Stone' to continue through light woodland with plenty of rhododendrons and a field rich in daffodils, wonderful in Spring. The Baden-Powell memorial stone is impressive; fork left here, downhill to see a boy scout 'trading post'.

Keep to this lower path, passing the former industrial area. The views to other islands and the mainland are better as the route is

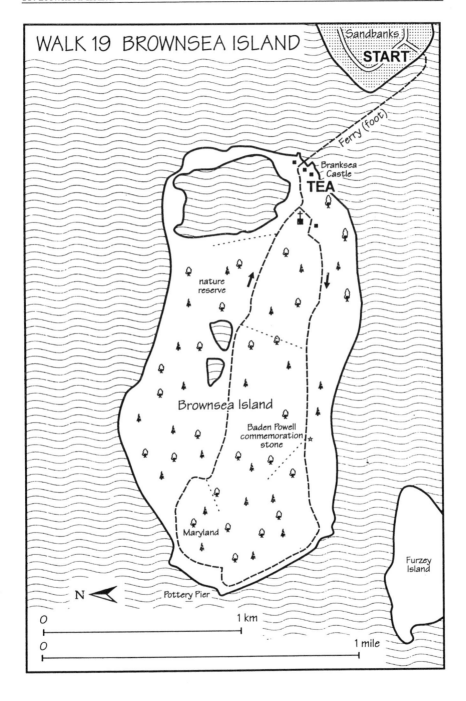

WALK 19 BROWNSEA ISLAND

Sandbanks
START

Ferry (foot)

Branksea Castle

TEA

nature reserve

Brownsea Island

Baden Powell commemoration stone

Maryland

Furzey Island

N

Pottery Pier

0   1 km

0   1 mile

now close to the shore. Reach Pottery Pier, the 'New Pier' of 1855. Turn right for a short climb, including some steps.

Join a major track and turn left, soon passing the scant remains of Maryland. Rise to a gate to pass through an area rich in Scots Pine. At a junction bear left at a signpost 'The Quay' to head back, passing the large brick wall of the former vinery before rejoining the outward route by the church.

20. Wareham

Length	3¾ miles
Summary	A very level walk around the flat alluvial land between the River Trent (Piddle) and River Frome, between Wareham and Poole Harbour. The walk may not be exciting but there is much of quiet interest, not least the abundant bird life. Generally good paths.
Car Parking	In Wareham town centre, behind the old town hall, pay and display. with public conveniences, grid reference 924874.
Maps	Ordnance Survey Outdoor Leisure no. 15, Purbeck and South Dorset, 1:25,000 or Landranger no. 195, Bournemouth and Purbeck, 1:50,000.

Tea Shop

There is a warm welcome for walkers at The Old Granary. Outside seating by the river is a lovely choice but on cooler days one may prefer one of the tables in the window of the restaurant overlooking the River Frome. Morning coffee, light lunches, afternoon teas, evening

The Old Granary tea shop

meals, are all served and the menu is very comprehensive. Service noticeably helpful and pleasant. Bed and breakfast also available. Open: Every day, all the year, 10am – 9pm – evening meals from 6pm. Tel. 01929 552010.

About the Area

The very old town of Wareham sits strategically across the main entrance to the distinctive Isle of Purbeck, close to the marshy fringe of Poole Harbour and embraced by the two rivers. The roughly north, south, east and west grid layout of the principal streets is of Roman origin. A fair length of the great earth rampart which was constructed by Alfred the Great to protect the town from Viking raiders on all but the south side, where the river is a barrier, is still evident.

At the north end the small church of St Martin's on the Wall has surviving Saxon features, including the chancel arch. An effigy of T.E. Lawrence ('of Arabia') was sculpted by Eric Kennington and donated by Lawrence's brother. There are also some fairly recently discovered pre-Reformation murals.

Much larger is St Mary's Church, a fine building at the south end of town, with stone relics of great interest and a rare lead font.

The town is very much the centre for a considerable area of south-east Dorset and is well provided with shops and other amenities, including a historic cinema. The attractive area by the former granary, beside the R. Frome, has a quay and boats for hire. Close by, in a converted church building, is the Purbeck Information and Heritage Centre. Across the river to the north is a separated part of Wareham, modern industrial/business/residential, including the railway station.

The Walk

Head for the main street, North Street, passing the public conveniences. Turn right, very soon reaching St Martin's Church, open for visitors during the summer season and with the key obtainable nearby at other times. Bear right at the church then left at a signpost into a residential road, then right at a junction to take a path ascending the grassy bank on the left, part of the ancient town rampart/wall.

The top of the rampart makes a fine elevated walk on short grass. By the end of a modern residential area turn left to go down the bank

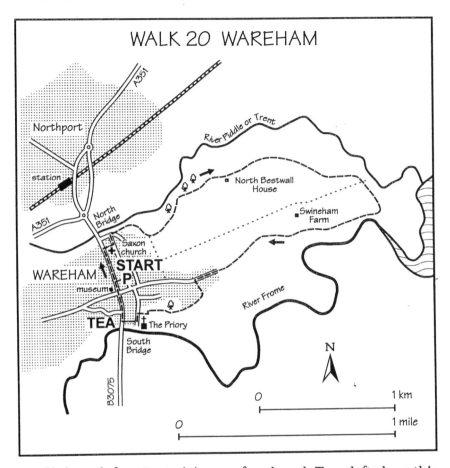

WALK 20 WAREHAM

on a little path for 10m to join a surfaced road. Turn left along this private road, with waymark and a warning about dogs chasing deer. The plentiful trees include a good deal of oak.

Pass the entrance to a gravel extraction area and continue to a waymarked gate. The private road goes to North Bestwall House, partly hidden by trees, Our path, now without surface, forks left through more woodland. Go over a gate/stile on the left to take a track along the edge of water meadows to a waymarked gate/stile. The railway embankment is in view across the river and wooded Arne Hill, all of 53m. high, is ahead. Much of the way here may be wet and cattle churned.

Go over a waymarked stile and bear right, close to the edge of the water of Poole Harbour.

For a short way back to Wareham, go over another waymarked stile to take a permissive path on the right.

To continue, bear left and then, in 20m, go to the right over a stile to follow a rather overgrown track between fences, close to the water. As boats moored on the R. Frome come into view, bear right again, soon by the river.

In a short distance, by a little inlet, there is another choice of route.

To the left is a little path which hugs the river bank all the way back to town, its weaving course adding about three-quarters of a mile to the overall distance. Unfortunately this path is largely overgrown.

Straight on is a bramble-lined grassy lane which becomes surfaced as the access drive to Swineham Farm is reached at a waymarked gate/stile. The long ridge of the Purbeck Hills forms the skyline to the left. The edge of the built-up residential area is soon reached; at a signpost 'footpath to river bank' in 200m turn left. Don't go the river bank but keep right at a point where the riverside route joins, to head towards St Mary's Church, reaching the roadway between the two parts of the cemetery.

Pass the church and turn left to the quay and the tea shop. The information and heritage centre is signposted, across the main street.

Return along the main street to the traffic lights, former town hall and car park.

21. Moreton and Bovington

Length	7½ miles
Summary	An almost level walk on good tracks, largely in woodland. At worst, a little mud. Much of the route is close to army activity. Rather more than half a mile by the side of public roads.
Car Parking	Roadside lay-by half a mile south of Lawrence's cottage, Clouds Hill, grid reference 827905.
Maps	Ordnance Survey Outdoor Leisure no. 15, Purbeck and South Dorset, 1:25,000 or Landranger no. 194, Dorchester and Weymouth, 1:50,000

Tea Shop

The cafeteria at the Tank Museum could not possibly be described as a charming tea shop – it is a large, rather utilitarian café. However it does provide a welcome refreshment stop part way round an interesting walk. A comprehensive choice of food and beverages is available at the self-service counter. Photographs of military vehicles are displayed on the walls.

Open: 10am – 4.30pm every day all the year. Tel. 01929 405096.

About the Area

The linking theme of this walk is T. E. Lawrence ('of Arabia') still widely esteemed as a scholar, soldier, writer and generally larger than life character of the early part of the present century. His activities with the Arabs in desert warfare against the Turks in World War I are legendary and are the subject of several books and an epic film. Although post World War II research has to some extent modified the schoolboy hero image, Lawrence remains as a fascinating and mysterious character.

His lonely cottage, Clouds Hill, set in deeply wooded surroundings, is a popular attraction. Owned by the National Trust, it is open to the public on Wednesday, Thursday, Friday, Sunday and Bank Holiday Mondays from 12 noon to 5pm or dusk if earlier (there is no electricity) from early April to the end of October.

Lawrence's grave at Moreton, the other end of this walk, also attracts many visitors.

The army has long had a considerable presence at Bovington, where the heathland has proved to be excellent for tank and armoured vehicle training. It is the natural situation for the Tank Museum, where the past 80 years of armoured warfare is thoroughly set out in documents and a large collection of exhibits including many tanks. The museum is open to the public daily from 10am until 5pm

Moreton is a tiny, off the beaten track, village with Lawrence's grave, a post office stores and St Nicholas's Church. After rebuilds in the 18th and 19th centuries, the church was damaged by a bomb in 1940. It was rebuilt again in 1950, using most of the original stone and the same design. The really celebrated feature is the wonderfully detailed etching of the glass of the windows by Lawrence Whistler. Explanations of the various scenes are set out in the church.

The tank museum, Bovington

The Walk

The car parking lay-by has boards with information about types of tank and armoured vehicle which may be seen on the adjoining test track. Leave the car park by a path in the northern corner, with yel-

low arrow waymark. The narrow path stays in the woodland between the road and the tank test track, not greatly used but always
distinct, the route among rhododendron and holly confirmed by
waymarks.

At a fork keep right, close to a fence. Reach a few steps and descend to the side of a public road. Turn left, then left again at a
nearby junction to walk to Clouds Hill Cottage if a visit is desired.
From the cottage return to the road junction and turn left to stay by
the roadside for almost a quarter of a mile. At a minor junction turn
left to leave the road along a broad forest track. This is Moreton
Drive, entered at a gate with a 'walkers welcome' logo.

The drive is almost straight, very slightly downhill through
Moreton Plantation. There are sweet chestnut trees by the trackside.
Ignore a waymarked right turn and go straight on, the track soon
having a hard surface. Close to the end of the woodland go straight
on at a junction.

A left turn here misses out Moreton and shortens the walk by about 1
mile.

Continue along a bramble-lined track towards Moreton village,
crossing a bridge and bearing right to reach a long footbridge beside
a ford across the R. Frome. Pass the village stores. St Nicholas's
Church is to the left. At a road junction keep left; the cemetery with
Lawrence's grave is a short distance further, on the right.

Return from Moreton initially by the same route, re-crossing the
river by the long footbridge, but turn right into a farm roadway at the
near edge of the woodland. The Hardy monument (ref. walk no. 11)
is visible on the skyline. Go left at the next junction, with waymark,
to take a good broad track, passing a lone house named 'The Glade'.

Cross a more open area before re-entering woodland, well varied
with silver birch, holly, rhododendron and conifers. Keep right at a
junction; the proximity to an army camp is obvious as a junction
with two sets of gates 'beware of military traffic' is reached. Continue along a very broad track to a gate with a waymark and the edge
of Bovington Camp. Go across Menin Road into a bramble-lined
footpath opposite, which continues in a straight line to the main
camp road. Turn right to follow the road as it bends to the left to the
Tank Museum; the refreshments are at the far end, on the right.

The shortest way back is to stay with the road, but the distance is more
than 1½ miles.

WALK 21 MORETON AND BOVINGTON

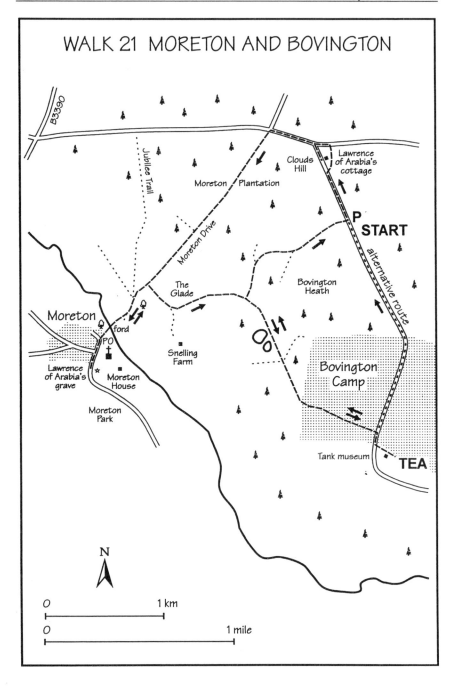

B3390

Jubilee Trail

Moreton Plantation

Clouds Hill

Lawrence of Arabia's cottage

P START

Moreton Drive

alternative route

The Glade

Bovington Heath

Moreton

ford

PO

Snelling Farm

Lawrence of Arabia's grave

Moreton House

Bovington Camp

Moreton Park

Tank museum

TEA

N

0   1 km

0   1 mile

It is more enjoyable to retrace part of the outward route. Look out for a 'Moreton' finger post at the start of the first footpath. Two hundred metres after the double gated junction, there is a short (no right of way ?) diversion to the left to see two very quiet and attractive lakes. Continue to the open area then, towards the far end, turn right, up-hill, at a major junction, with another Forest Enterprises 'walkers welcome' sign. The gradient, ascending to Bovington Heath, is never steep as it rises through the woodland. Keep right at any junction.

Emerge by the side of a tank training area and follow a well waymarked path to a stile and the public road almost opposite the car park.

22. Bradford Peverell

Length	3 miles
Summary	A gentle little walk in quietly attractive countryside, without problems of navigation and without the adventure of crossing fields with ploughed over paths and/or overgrown stiles. In short, a pleasant ramble.
Car Parking	Informal, by the church in Bradford Peverell, at the foot of the lane which leads to the New Barn Field Centre, grid reference 659930.
Maps	Ordnance Survey Outdoor Leisure no. 15, Purbeck and South Dorset, 1:25,000 or Explorer no. 117, Cerne Abbas and Bere Regis, 1:25,000 or Landranger no. 194, Dorchester and Weymouth, 1:50,000.

Tea Shop

New Barn, whilst welcoming visitors enthusiastically, is principally a residential study centre for school and student groups. The whole enterprise is immaculate with interesting conversions of 18th century barns, stables, and cart sheds as well as farm cottages. Amongst other attractions, paying visitors can see the Iron Age homestead, exhibition of bygones, nature trail, and the wild flower reserve. However, for the purpose of this book, the coffee shop can be accessed without an admission charge and walkers are very welcome. In fact it would be a great pity to miss this café – it is smart, clean, and inviting with cheerful decor, boot-friendly tiled floor and sturdy wooden furniture. John, the catering manager for the field centre, is an enthusiast and is justifiably proud of the menu. His home-made cakes are simply delicious – strongly recommend the carrot cake! Sandwiches are freshly made and also available is a very good quiche served with salad garnish. Drinks include glasses of milk, apple juice, citron or elderflower presse – all from the chiller cabinet; plus good quality coffee and tea. Cream teas are served every day. Cooked lunches on Sundays available by reservation only.
Open: 10am to 5pm every day from the week before Easter to the end of September. The remainder of the year will vary depending on residential occupancy – you are welcome to telephone first or to take a chance! Tel. 01305 267463

About the Area

Situated in the broad valley of the R. Frome, just off the A37, Dorchester to Yeovil road, 3 miles north-west of Dorchester, Bradford Peverell is a pleasant but unremarkable village. Likewise the surrounding countryside is undulating but without any of the more striking hill formations found in other parts of the county.

On the Bradford side of the valley there are several places where traces of a Roman aqueduct may be found. It carried considerable quantities of water for 12 miles from Notton Mill near Maiden Newton to Dorchester, with an overall fall of less than 8m (about 25ft.).

The New Barn Field Centre helps the visitor to discover what life was really like for our distant ancestors of up to 2,000 years ago. Additionally there is a pottery, a wild flower reserve, a nature trail and farm animals. The centre is open throughout the year.

Nearby Dorchester is the Dorset county town, with the full range of expected facilities, including two railway stations and several museums. Most important is the connection with the great novelist Thomas Hardy whose 'Casterbridge' the town is; Max Gate (National Trust) was his home for more than 40 years.

New Barn Field Centre

The Walk

The unsurfaced roadway which leaves the village street in Bradford Peverell is well signposted to the New Barn Field Centre. Walk up this roadway, passing large quantities of scrap agricultural and other machinery. Fork right in about quarter of a mile on to a tree-shaded bridleway rising gently along Strap Bottom.

Go through a waymarked gate and along the edge of a field to a waymarked double gate. Carry on. There are good long views of the rich, rolling, Dorset countryside; across the valley of the R. Frome Pen Hill reaches a height of just over 140m (459ft.)

Turn left through a gate at a junction of paths, again following a blue bridleway waymark. The broad track passes new tree planting on the left before reaching a junction. Turn right here to continue through woodland which has beech, sycamore and conifers. Emerge from the woodland and continue, slightly downhill.

Follow a waymark on a tree to go left between agricultural buildings, some of them huge, and past a row of cottages at Lower Skippet Farm. Re-enter woodland, turning right at a junction to walk down a narrow tree belt. More then half way down turn left through a gate; this junction is well supplied with waymarks.

Another excellent track keeps close to the left edge of a huge field, generally rising. To the right is Combe Bottom. Ahead is a clump of trees through which parts of the New Barn Field Centre complex can be seen. Reach a rough roadway and turn right, soon arriving at New Barn and refreshments.

After the break turn left to continue along the New Barn access roadway. In 150m, as the road bends to the left, a right of way to the village goes straight through a double farm gate and across a large descending field, aiming roughly mid-way between the church steeple and the right-hand field boundary. If crops obscure this route, as is likely, follow the roadway back to the parking place.

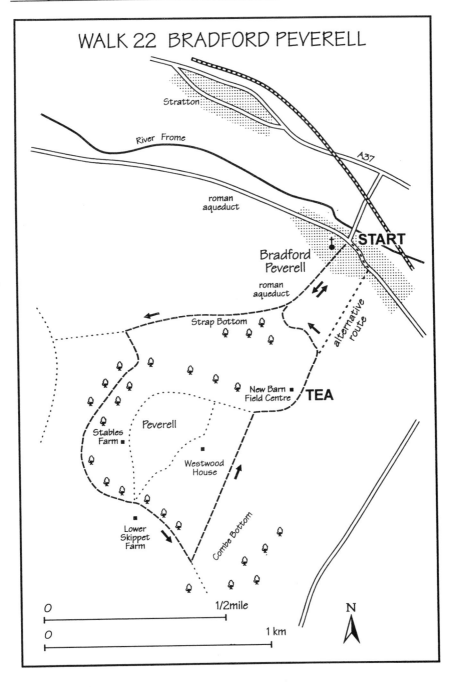

WALK 22 BRADFORD PEVERELL

Stratton

River Frome

A37

roman
aqueduct

START

Bradford
Peverell

roman
aqueduct

Strap Bottom

alternative
route

New Barn
Field Centre
TEA

Peverell

Stables
Farm

Westwood
House

Lower
Skippet
Farm

Combe Bottom

0   1/2mile
0   1 km

N

23. Cerne Abbas and Minterne Magna

Length	5½ miles
Summary	A circuit based on the most attractive and interesting village of Cerne Abbas, starting and finishing at the smaller village of Minterne Magna. This is largely downland walking, good underfoot, with very little on public roads.
Car Parking	Car park by the side of the A352, opposite the church in Minterne Magna, grid reference 659043. There are information boards but no public conveniences.
Maps	Ordnance Survey Explorer no. 117, Cerne Abbas and Bere Regis, 1:25,000 or Landranger no. 194, Dorchester and Weymouth, 1:50,000

Tea Shop

Part way round the walk we were delighted to find "The Old Market House" right in the centre of Cerne Abbas – a peaceful and unspoilt village. In fact it would be hard to resist visiting this tea room – the decor is very pleasing with draped curtains and tablecloths made from the same material. The cakes table is laden with slices of temptations such as banana and chocolate loaf, carrot cake, sponge sandwich cake, and many other choices. Excellent cream teas are served. Try smoked mackerel and apple salad or grilled goats' cheese with a salad garnish – the crab sandwiches were super too! Some tables outside.

Open: 10am – 5pm. Always closed on Tuesdays. In winter months open weekends only. Tel. 01300 341680.

About the Area

It is no exaggeration to say that Cerne Abbas is one of Dorset's finest villages. Praise indeed in a county which prides itself on the excellence of its villages. Many of the houses are 18th century, but the terrace facing the church is much older, forming one side of a wonderfully pretty street.

The church is 15th century, with a fine tower. A rare survival is the little Madonna and child in a niche in the tower; one of only a few in England which survived the iconoclasm of the Reformation and the enthusiasm of Cromwell's men for destroying church ornamentation. Close by was Cerne Abbey, founded more than 1,000 years ago by the great Saxon scholar Alfric, who became first Abbot. Only fragments of the Abbey remain, including a three storey gatehouse, the guest house and a 15th century tithe barn. There is now a pottery by the ruins.

Also notable in this ancient place is St Augustine's Well, accessed through the churchyard. According to legend, this well was created by St Augustine on his 6th century mission to convert the English. Fed by a powerful spring, the well was probably believed to have curative powers. There are carved stones in the surrounding structure.

Despite this array of historic features, however, widespread public awareness of Cerne Abbas centres on just one, very prominent, piece of ancient history – the Cerne Abbas Giant, cut into the chalk and flaunting himself shamelessly on a bare hillside. His age is un-

The Cerne Abbas giant

known, but could well be pre Roman. Another suggestion is that he depicts a Saxon god, presumably of fertility. His overall size is enormous, about the height of 30 tall men, and other measurements are likewise impressive; for example the club which he carries is more than 36m (120ft.) long and his phallus, at 7.2m. (23ft.) is of disproportionate size.

Minterne Magna is little more than a farming hamlet, but there is a church which is more than 400 years old. Beside the church is the entrance to the gardens of Minterne House. Landscaped in the 18th century along a valley side, the gardens have lakes, cascades and streams, with rare trees and shrubs and autumn colouring. Open to the public from late March to early November, Monday to Saturday, 10am to 7pm

The Walk

From the car park cross the road to take a broad, stony, track on the near side of the church signposted 'bridleway Buckland Newton 2'. Cross a tiny stream on a footbridge and bear right to start the ascent of the valley side. Go through a waymarked gate and rise along the edge of a road to a signpost, bearing left here to follow the blue waymark.

After a little gate keep to a well-marked path across a cultivated field. After two more gates (one possibly missing), go diagonally to the right across a field to a waymarked gate and continue towards woodland on a path which is now not entirely obvious on the ground. The proximity to the top of the ridge provides long views to the right, including Cerne Abbas and its area.

Turn left at a waymarked post to go to a gate giving access to a major track. Turn right to walk along the top edge of woodland. Through occasional gaps in the hedge there are views over the countryside to the left. On reaching a meeting place of tracks towards the far end of the wood take care; turn right at the second opportunity, through a small metal gate to continue along the top of the scarp, with a fence on the right and some woodland below.

The path is faint but this is good downland walking, rising gently, and accompanied by the song of birds, including skylarks. There are clumps of gorse as the track approaches more woodland, angling towards a public road. Immediately before the road turn right to go downhill, not initially into the wood. The visible path threads its

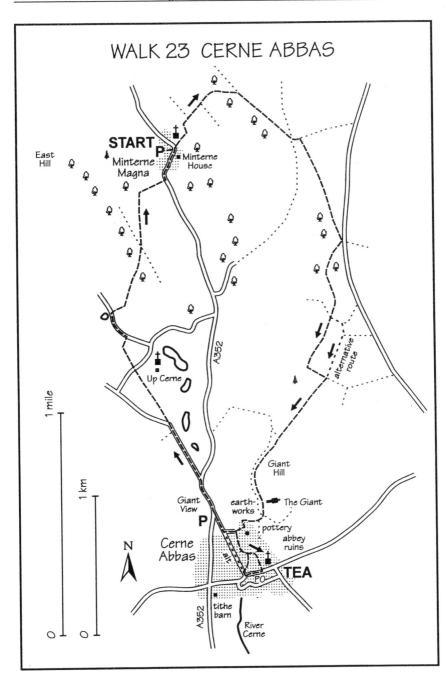

WALK 23 CERNE ABBAS

way gently down, soon bending left to traverse a wood rich in blue-bells in Spring.

The wood is followed by more open hillside, with clumps of gorse. Another bridleway crosses our route; there is a choice here. Either turn left, uphill, for rather more than 100m and then turn right at a footpath or keep straight on for a further 1/3 mile on a net-tle-impinged path, then turn left uphill to a waymarked farm gate and along the edge of a field to join the same footpath at a signpost.

In either case from the signpost cross the large cultivated field ahead, probably helped by farm wheel tracks, to a waymarked stile at the far side. Continue along a grassy path, soon descending among undergrowth before emerging on to the open hillside. Pass below the Giant, along the parallel grooves of a long ago inhabited area, now rich in cowslips. Only the feet are visible from below.

Descend a steep bank down to a track at the bottom, turn right and take the first stile on the right to follow a rather overgrown track leading to an agricultural building. Turn left. Ahead is a veterinary practice, the pottery, and evidence of the former Abbey, but turn right in 40m, cross a substantial bridge over the R. Cerney, and turn left along a riverside footpath. This path leads into the village; keep left at two junctions to reach the lovely street by the church. The tea shop is unmissable at the end of this street, to the right.

To see more of the village walk along the street to the west and turn right to follow the minor road up to the Giant's View car park by the side of the main road.

A preferred alternative is to turn right by the Singing Kettle, then right again into Mill Lane to rejoin the route used into the village along the side of the river. At the far end turn left, pass a picnic area, and rise to the Giant's View car park.

Having admired the Giant, walk along the side of the main road, passing a nursing home. In a further 70m fork left into a very minor road signposted 'Up Cerne 1'. The little road is pleasant to walk, gently uphill. Below, to the right, are ornamental lakes, rich in wa-terfowl. As the road bends to the left, go straight on at a waymarked gate/stile between two large horse-chestnut trees. The path goes clearly across a cultivated field towards a gate at the far side.

Cross the minor road and follow wheel tracks through another cultivated field. At the far end of a few trees bear right to go down to the road. Turn left to walk along the road for 200m or so, accompa-nied by a clear-flowing brook. Opposite a dwelling set back in wooded grounds, turn right at a signposted bridleway, rising into woodland. This excellent track climbs steadily to the top of Farm Hill. Bear left at the top and then immediately turn right, through the hedge, to take a downhill path. In about 40m, opposite a wide gap in the hedge on the right, turn left to go diagonally across a field, possibly helped by farm wheel tracks, to a farm gate on the right. Continue the same line, with some of Minterne Magna now in view ahead, across a pathless meadow to a wide gap in the fence at the bottom right corner. There is a chalk pit to the left.

Turn right, go through a gate, to continue along a fine avenue, mainly of beeches, to a gate giving access to the A352. Turn left to return to the church and car park, possibly trying to count the number of chimney stacks at Minterne House, to the right.

```
┌─────────────────────────────────────────────────────┐
│ ┌─────────────────────────────────────────────────┐ │
│ │                                                 │ │
│ │            24. Milton Abbas                     │ │
│ │                                                 │ │
│ └─────────────────────────────────────────────────┘ │
└─────────────────────────────────────────────────────┘
```

Length	3 miles
Summary	An easy walk with many interesting features, linking Milton Abbey, St Catherine's Chapel and the 'new' village of Milton Abbas. Entirely straightforward and very good underfoot.
Car Parking	Informal roadside area for 5 or 6 cars on the minor road from Milton Abbas to Milton Abbey School and Hilton, at the point where the track to St Catherine's Chapel leaves the road, grid reference 802021.
Map	Ordnance Survey Explorer no. 117, Cerne Abbas and Bere Regis, 1:25,000 or Landranger no. 194, Dorchester and Weymouth, 1:50,000

Tea Shop

The chosen venue provides a welcome break part way round this delightful walk. "The Tea Clipper" serves morning coffee, light lunches, and for tea one may find some difficulty choosing from all the delectable cakes displayed on the sideboard. We sampled buttered apricot and sultana bread and the Bakewell tart – both were mouth-watering. Also displayed were iced carrot cake, chocolate sponge and Dorset apple cake. Other items for tea are the scones served with cream and jam. All the cakes and scones are made on the premises and there was a delicious smell of home cooking when we were there. For something savoury there are sandwiches, toasted sandwiches, jacket potatoes, and some cooked dishes are offered. Drinks include tea with milk or lemon, speciality teas, coffee, hot chocolate, and glasses of milk. The tea room is attractive and has a gift shop at one end. For sunny days there is a sheltered courtyard with tables and benches.

Open: 10.30am – 5pm daily from Easter to the end of October but closed on Mondays. Tel. 01258 880223.

About the Area

Milton Abbas is an unusual place; a 'model' village built in the late 18th century by the 1st. Earl of Dorchester, when he demolished the existing town because he disliked the smell and the noise in close proximity to the splendid mansion which he was then constructing close to the remains of the Abbey. The new village was some distance away, along the bottom of a descending valley. The well-spaced identical houses faced each other across a wide street. Although there have been subsequent modifications, the regularity is still very marked, varied by the village church, the post office/stores, the tea shop and the inn.

In 933 a Benedictine Abbey was founded at Milton by Athelstan, first king of the whole of England. Rebuilt in the 14th and 15th centuries, the Abbey church has survived both the Dissolution and the general destruction of the 18th century. Indeed, the Earl took care to ensure that his house matched the Abbey church. Similar to a small cathedral, the church is full of interesting features.

The abbey at Milton Abbas

Milton Abbey School now occupies the mansion buildings; the grounds and playing fields surround both mansion and Abbey church. From the grounds a remarkable stairway of 111 turf steps leads up towards St Catherine's Chapel.

High in the nearby woods, this little 12th century Chapel is quite charming. The legend is that Athelstan and his men camped here on the way to confront the invading Danes in the north. Athelstan had a

vision of victory and, when this was duly fulfilled, he later returned
to found the Abbey in gratitude. In the middle ages, the chapel was a
last stopping place for pilgrims en route for the Abbey; according to a
plaque beside the door, indulgences were automatically granted to
the penitents. It would be pleasant to think that genuine walkers
could also qualify!

The Walk

Start along the broad, unsurfaced, roadway, uphill into the woods,
signposted '12th century chapel 1st. left'. Turn sharp left, as ad-
vised, in about 100m and continue easily to reach the chapel, a
pleasing little structure with one or two interesting features, not
least the 120 day indulgence for pilgrims. The view down to Milton
Abbey is very fine.

After the chapel carry on uphill through the woodland. Turn left
at a 'T' junction on to another forest track. Initially level, this track
rises after a junction. The managed forest is quite diverse, with
plenty of beech, ash and sycamore. As the woodland opens out, red
campion and other wild flowers grow well.

Reach an area where several tracks join, close to houses; go left for
15m. and then right through large ornamental gates, along a driveway. In 30m turn right to follow a bridleway; there is a
well-concealed waymark here. The bridleway is well marked along
the edge of a huge field. Go through a little gate as an estate of houses
is approached. This is the area in which the Ordnance Survey places
'St Catherine's Well'.

Bear left to another little gate, with waymark, and a path beside a
house, leading to a surfaced road. Go left along the road, turning
right in 50m on a grass track beside a children's play area. The path
continues between older houses. Cross a roadway and turn right for
a few metres, then left down another road, with a 'public bridleway'
sign. Bear right in a few metres to take a stony lane, then go left down
a well-shaded track, part of the 'Jubilee Trail', downhill, helped by a
few broad, shallow, steps, with a canopy of beech, ash and sycamore.

Emerge from this convoluted little section high up the main street
of Milton Abbas village and turn right to descend past the post of-
fice/stores and the Hambro Arms Inn to the tea shop.

After refreshment continue down the street. Turn right at the bot-

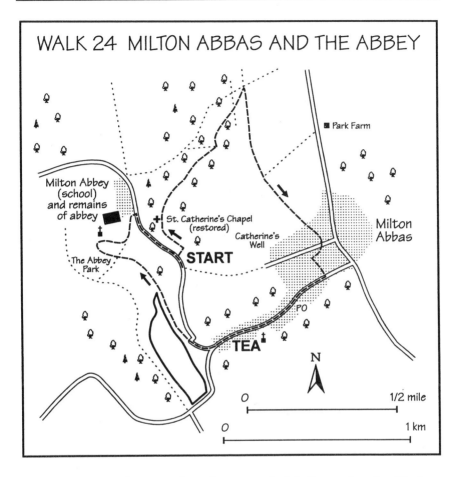

WALK 24 MILTON ABBAS AND THE ABBEY

tom at a 'Hilton' signpost then, in 100m, fork left at a thatched lodge, signposted 'public footpath to Milton Abbey Church only'. This path is known locally as the 'Monks Path'. It winds beside the lake, leading to the west door of the Abbey church. School grounds are crossed on the way and visitors are requested to keep to the path, which is the only right of way.

However, after viewing the church take a gravel path along the south side of the church (away from the school buildings), reach a surfaced drive and turn left to a school access and car parking area. Turn right up a vehicular 'no access' road to the public road. Turn right to return uphill to the parking area in 250m, passing under a large arch in 50m.

---

25. Kingston Lacy and
Badbury Rings

Length	2 miles (Kingston Lacy)
Summary	This walk is basically within the grounds of Kingston Lacy, a stately home owned and managed by the National Trust. The walk is level and very easy, through woodland and gardens, excellent underfoot. Except for members of the N.T. there is, of course, an admission charge. Whilst this walk is self-contained, for those with time (and possibly energy) to spare, there is an interesting and contrasting walk over Badbury Rings less than two miles down the road. Here there is easy walking over sheep-grazed grass. Dogs are not admitted.
Car Parking	At Kingston Lacy, grid reference 978014. At Badbury Rings, just off B3082, grid reference 960032.
Maps	Ordnance Survey Explorer no. 118, Shaftesbury and Cranbourne Chase, 1:25,000 or Landranger no. 195, Bournemouth and Poole, 1:50,000.

Tea Shop

The tea rooms at Kingston Lacey are housed in the large stable block. In accordance with National Trust policy as little as possible has been altered; the stalls make divisions, each holding three or four tables to seat four, the brick floor has been retained and there are items of saddlery around. Furniture is modern made of good quality wood and the tables have attractive vinyl covers. The lack of fabric to absorb noise does affect the acoustics but this is really only a small point. Counter service with a good selection of food and drink is available all day. If having a main course, why not try National Trust own-label wine? Cream teas always available and of good quality. Open: 1st April/Easter to end of October from 11.30am – 5pm every day. Also open on Fridays, Saturdays and Sundays in November and December from 11am – 4pm. Tel. 01202 889242.

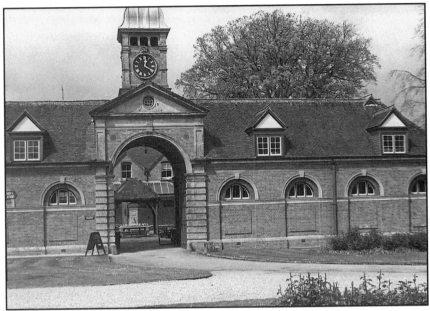

The tea rooms at Kingston Lacy

About the Area

The Kingston Lacy estate was bought by Sir John Bankes in 1632-6. Sir Ralph Bankes built the house in the 1660s after the Civil War had brought about the destruction of the family seat at Corfe Castle. The architect was Roger Pratt; his red brick construction was remodelled inside in the 1780s. Between 1835 and 1841 William Bankes, a much travelled man, commissioned Charles Barry (of Houses of Parliament fame) to transform Kingston Lacy into the style of a 17th century Italian palazzo, clad in grey-green Chilmark stone, as we see it today. William brought back many treasures from his travels, including the obelisk from Philae which has helped scholars to understand Egyptian hieroglyphs.

The stables date from 1880 and the restored Victorian fernery re-uses stone from some of the earlier buildings on the site.

Badbury Rings is one of the larger and more important of the Dorset iron age hill forts, constructed over a long period from the 6th century BC to the 1st century A.D. The line of a Roman road crosses the site.

Less than two miles from Kingston Lacy is Wimborne Minster, a small town with a great treasure house in the Minster itself. Wimborne also has several more modern visitor attractions such as Priest's House Museum, a model town and gardens and Walford Mill.

The Walk

From the parking area walk back along the exit driveway, away from the house. As the drive bends to the right, about 150m from the information building, turn left through a small waymarked gate. Go over grass along the edge of a meadow.

Go through a gate into woodland to a signpost. Turn left to follow 'woodland trail and dog walk 2 miles' The excellent track is always broad and predominantly level; the waymarking is thorough and must be followed.

The woodland is well varied and, in Spring, bluebells, red campion, ramsoms, primroses and others are abundant along the way, as is bird life. At a semi-clearing there are two unusual and creative wood benches. The house is visible to the left as a driveway is crossed via two gates. From this area an obelisk and the herd of beautifully coloured Red Devon cattle can usually be seen.

A second monument soon becomes visible; at a 'T' junction there is a short way back to the house for those not accompanied by a dog. Turn right to continue the 'woodland trail'. Go straight on as a garden area is reached, passing profuse azaleas and rhododendrons, then two pet animal gravestones and an avenue of cedars, always keeping to the waymarked route.

Go through a small iron gate and across grass towards the side of the house, bearing right to reach the surfaced front drive and return to the car park. The Stables Restaurant is accessed via a gate on the left.

Badbury Rings

For this option, from Kingston Lacy turn left along the B3182 towards Blandford Forum, then turn right at a 'Badbury Rings' signpost in less than two miles into an unsurfaced road to find the parking area recommended above. Towards the far end of this area there is an information board.

There are several rights of way which can be used to make a circu-

WALK 25 KINGSTON LACY AND BADBURY RINGS

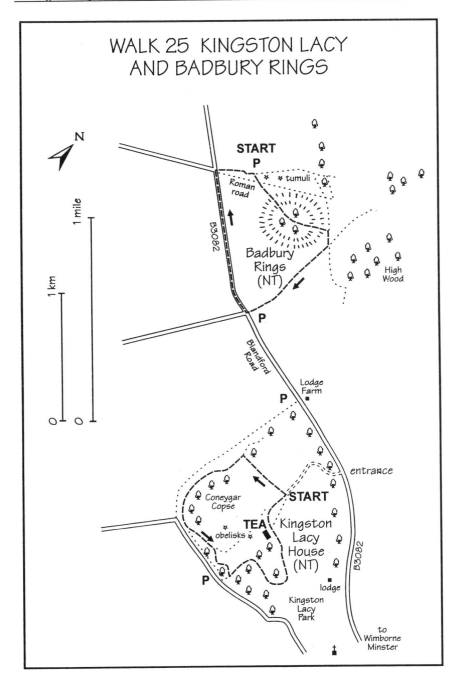

lar walk of up to three miles or so, including a track along the wide grassy area which flanks the B3082 road, behind the great row of beeches. There are said to be 365 of these trees, one for each day of the year, making a fine avenue.

For a modest walk of about two miles, go through the gate and head straight across N.T. land for the tree-clad summit, crossing the Roman alignment in a few metres. At the first 'ring', a made path starts. Go to a direction viewpoint on top, now partly nullified by the growth of trees.

Continue straight on to the inner 'ring', turning right to reach a trig. point. At the next dip go left to a gate at the edge of woodland and join a track, turning right. Turn right again at a junction of tracks and follow a field boundary down to the road. Turn right to walk behind the avenue of beech trees back to the unmade roadway which leads to the car park.

Alternatively, select your 'ring' and circumnavigate the fort, for a mini walk of about a mile.

26. Shaftesbury

Length	4 miles
Summary	A comparatively gentle walk through Shaftesbury and in the adjacent countryside. Some mud is possible and one cultivated field may well be awkward.
Car Parking	Pay and display car park with public conveniences at Bell Street in town centre, close to Tourist Information Centre, grid reference 861231.
Maps	Ordnance Survey Explorer no. 118, Shaftesbury and Cranbourne Chase, 1:25,000 or Landranger no. 183, Yeovil and Frome, 1:50,000.

Tea Shop

They certainly don't burn the cakes these days in "King Alfred's Kitchen". This popular "olde world tea shop" is situated right in the centre of Shaftesbury and offers well presented food. There are two beamed tea rooms – one down and one up from the entrance. The waitress service is most pleasant and efficient. A variety of teas is available and coffees offered include percolated, espresso, or cappuccino. Other drinks are Horlicks, Bovril and cold drinks. Savouries range from healthy salads, mushrooms on toast, to sausage and chips; the special menu for children even offers Marmite soldiers! As usual a cream tea is available; and for a change why not try cinnamon toast?
Open: 9.15am – 5pm every day (almost!) of the year but not on Christmas Day. Tel. 01747 852147.

About the Area

Well to the north of the county, facing south over the expanse of Blackmore Vale, Shaftesbury is a fine little town, steeped in history. This was Alfred the Great's town; he was responsible for the foundation of the Abbey, set up as a Benedictine Nunnery, with his daughter as first Abbess. It is claimed that the body of the unfortunate St Edward was brought here after his murder at Corfe Castle in 979 and that in 1038 King Canute died of a heart attack whilst praying at Edward's shrine.

Centuries later, stone of the Abbey was used to construct much of what we see as the present town. During more recent times, excavation has revealed a great deal which assists in reconstructing the history of the Abbey; the grounds and on-site museum are open to the public seven days a week from Easter to the end of September. A charge is made. Access is from a lane which is signposted at the west end of High Street.

St Peter's is the most ancient of the town churches. Centrally situated beside the Town Hall, the church was connected by a passage to an adjacent inn. The age of the Town Hall reminds us that Shaftesbury was an ancient borough, with the office of Mayor dating back for many centuries. Of the many attractive old streets, pride of place goes to Gold Hill, with its curving terraces of lovely old houses falling away down the scarp; surely the finest street in Dorset.

Modern facilities include a Tourist Information Centre and the Shaftesbury Leisure Centre, found on Salisbury Road.

The Walk

Leave the car park beside Somerfield's supermarket and turn left along Bell Street (name sign not apparent). Continue past the public library; the street becomes Barton Hill, soon reaching the A30 main road near the fire station.

Cross the road, turn right then, in a few metres, turn left along Wincombe Lane, a cul de sac road. The lane soon leaves the built-up area, passing a school before reaching open countryside. At a junction keep left to head for Wincombe Farm. Go through the farm complex on a descending grass track, then along the bottom edge of woodland.

Turn left at a junction of tracks, with a lake just in view ahead and an area rich in rhododendron. Go through a gate and into a meadow, with a grand house, Winchcombe Park, well displayed at the top of the slope ahead. The right of way across the meadow angles away from the lake but passes well below the house, not obvious on the ground. It is probably preferable to stay lower down the slope than the Ordnance Survey indicates; the objective is to join an old sunken lane at the far end, then turning right to descend towards woodland.

Go through a gate at the bottom, passing a horse-churned section,

WALK 26 SHAFTESBURY

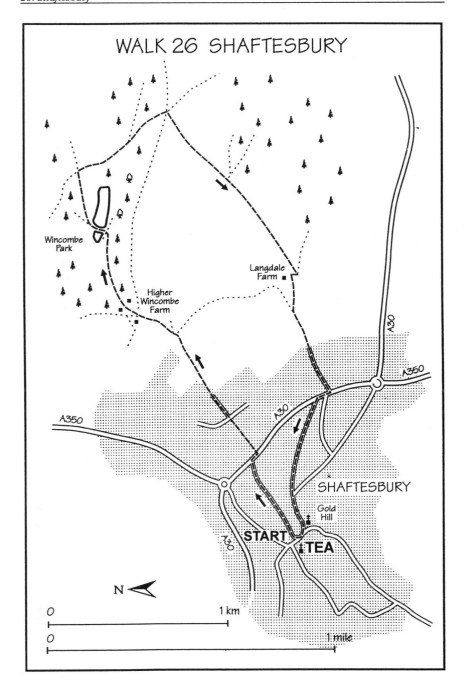

Wincombe
Park

Langdale
Farm

Higher
Wincombe
Farm

A30

A350

A350

A30

SHAFTESBURY

A30

Gold
Hill

START TEA

N

0   1 km

0   1 mile

and rise diagonally up the valley side, through Great Hanging Woods. Ignore any side paths. Emerge from the woods at the top of the slope at a meeting point of tracks. Go ahead to a waymarked gate and cross a large cultivated field, possibly with some difficulty. The direction is almost exactly south-west and the objective is the far left corner of the field, where a stile soon comes into view.

Go over two stiles and continue along the edge of a meadow, with a fence close to the right hand. After another stile, pass a property surrounded by a substantial brick wall. This has the appearance of an ex-MoD. depot. Continue by a hedge on the right to Langdale Farm.

The next two gate/stiles have 'Hardy Way' waymarks. Go over grass towards the corner of the farm garden and on to a stile on the right giving access to the farm road. Turn left to walk directly to the main A30 road, Christy's Lane, passing a cemetery on the way.

Turn right, then take the second turning on the left, Coppice Street, a quiet road rising back into the town, past a large free car park with camping/caravan site. At the road junction by the post office, go straight on to reach the tea shop, passing St Peter's Church and the old town hall. The car park is a few metres further.

Gold Hill, Shaftesbury

27. Sturminster Newton

Length	6 miles
Summary	A good circuit based on the attractive little town of Sturminster Newton, visiting two historic water mill sites and the top of the nearby Banbury Hill. Not too hilly and mostly good underfoot, but with some mud likely and the odd field ploughed too close to the boundary. Approximately half a mile along the side of a minor road.
Car Parking	At the historic mill site half a mile south of the town centre, off the A357. Public conveniences and picnic area. Grid reference 782135.
Maps	Ordnance Survey Explorer no. 129, Yeovil and Sherborne, 1:25,000 or Landranger no. 194, Dorchester and Weymouth, 1:50,000

Tea Shop

The chosen venue is Poets Corner Café. Turkish owner Yasar and his English wife, Becky, had been open for only about twelve months at the time of our visit and deserve to succeed with this café which is situated slightly off centre in Sturminster Newton. The decor is a mixture of Turkish and English. Excellent coffee, choice of teas including lemon, herb, or Earl Grey. Selection of cakes – especially delicious was the Turkish Baklava. More substantial fare is offered too – sausage and mash, mousaka, pasta dishes, all day English breakfast, and ploughman's lunch. Very reasonable prices and pleasant service. Genuine Turkish Delight is sold here.
Open: 9am – 5pm Mon – Sat and 10am – 4pm on Sundays all the year. Tel. 01258 473723.

About the Area

Of Roman origins and with the site of a Saxon Castle, the ancient little market town of Sturminster Newton, Hardy's 'Stourcastle', is set among the rolling countryside of Blackmore Vale. From the south the town is entered over a 15th century six arch bridge, widened in the following century. The bridge carries a plaque warning that fel-

Sturminster Newton Mill

ons who damage the bridge will be punished by transportation to Australia.

Close by is Sturminster Newton Mill, a working 17th century water mill open to the public from Easter to September, 11am to 5pm Monday, Thursday, Saturday and Sunday. Also in this outlying part of the town is the thatched 17th century Bull Inn.

In the main part of the town there is a local museum housed in a former workhouse chapel in Bath Road. The town centre itself comprises a cluster of old buildings, mostly post 1729, when there was a disastrous fire, with a central market cross of which only the octagonal base, probably 15th century, survives. The White Hart Inn, built in 1708, did somehow survive the fire.

William Barnes, a schoolmaster, poet and parson was born in Sturminster at the beginning of the 19th century, whilst the great Thomas Hardy lived here from 1876 to 1878 in a house at 'Riverside', along a minor road which leaves the A357 close to the mill. The 'Return of the Native' was written here.

One of the best loved of the slightly eccentric cross country railways of Britain was the Somerset and Dorset Joint Railway, which passed through Sturminster, with a centrally located station. Under the joint ownership of two major railway companies this line retained a great deal of independence until post World War II nationalisation. Basic services were from Bristol and Bath to Bournemouth, supplemented by a fair number of long distance holiday trains from the Midlands and North. The 'Pines Express' from Manchester was probably the best known of these trains. To great local and national dismay the line closed in 1966.

The Walk

Walk back up the mill access roadway to the A357. Turn left towards the town bridge then, just before the bridge, turn right at a raked back tarmac track signposted 'Hole House Lane ½' to rise past a Methodist church of 1870.

The route soon becomes a waymarked footpath, turning left up steps to avoid a dangerous section. Go over a stile and along the edge of a small field, then over another stile to a signpost by a gate. Head for 'Hole House Lane ¼'. The well-marked path is over grass along the edge of a large field. There is another stile as the edge of woodland on the left is reached, with plenty of bluebells.

At a very minor surfaced roadway turn right for 10m and then left to go over a stile at a 'Rudge Hill Farm ¾' signpost. The way is now very obvious; the settlement to the right is Glue Hill. The path continues along the edge of a field, soon swinging left to head south to a waymarked stile.

Go straight on, rising gently across rougher pasture, aiming for the left-hand edge of a small wood. The village to the left is Broad Oak. Pass a signpost 'Gipsy's Drove ¼'. When the Drove is reached at a potentially muddy junction close to a farm, turn left at a 'Gipsy's Drove and Dirty Gate' signpost.

Follow the old drove road for about half a mile in a fairly straight line, wheel-churned in places but otherwise reasonable underfoot. A short distance after crossing a dip, reach a meeting place of tracks, with a signpost. Turn right to follow a waymarked bridleway to 'Angers Lane ½'. The enclosed track is a little overgrown, but ignore the brambles and the mud and enjoy the wild flowers which include bluebells, early purple orchids and primroses.

Emerge from the woodland to follow a path worn on the grass close to the hedge on the left of a large meadow. As the hedge finishes turn sharp left, keeping another hedge on the left hand, rising towards an obvious waymarked gate. Go through and along a lane-like track, which soon has good views from its modest elevation. The top of Banbury Hill, not very exiting despite its hill fort, is immediately to the right.

Descend to the public road, Angers Lane, and go ahead to Banbury Cross (not the famous one!). Continue along the road.

Just after passing the last building on the left, turn left over a sign-posted stile 'Fiddleford A357 ¾'. Cross a field to a large opening in the hedge. The right of way goes diagonally across the next large, rising, field, to the top left corner, by Piddles Wood but, as the farmer seems to grow crops with no regard for walkers, it may be preferable to keep close to the hedge on the right; in some places even this may be found to be ploughed too close to the boundary.

Go through a broad gap in the fence (there is also a stile) to reach a signpost in 40m Continue towards 'Fiddleford ½' descending over grass by the side of a field. Go over a stile to the public road by a telephone box. Turn right, cross a stream on the road bridge and turn left at the Fiddleford Inn. The attractive beer garden may prove to be a distraction here.

Fork left 40m after the inn into a little lane which soon becomes a footpath, a walker's Fiddleford bypass. Rejoin the road, turning left towards Fiddleford Mill. Go straight ahead at a junction with a 'Sturminster Newton 1' sign and through the mill to footbridges over the River Stour, with sluices and large outfall weir. The mill house is a fine old building, marred only by some unfortunate roof re-covering.

On the far side of the river there is a choice of route back to Sturminster. A path across the intervening fields is a little shorter and more direct.

Perhaps more unusual is our route along the former railway line, reached by turning right by the side of the river, across lush riverside meadows. On reaching the piers of the dismantled railway bridge, go over a stile and turn left to follow the track-bed all the way to Sturminster, straight and slightly rising.

The line terminates at a large car park beside a small supermarket. Go to the pedestrian exit at the top. The tea shop is opposite, in Station Road.

From the tea shop carry on to Bath Road, cross by Barclay's Bank, and turn left to walk past The Square, with the base of the old market

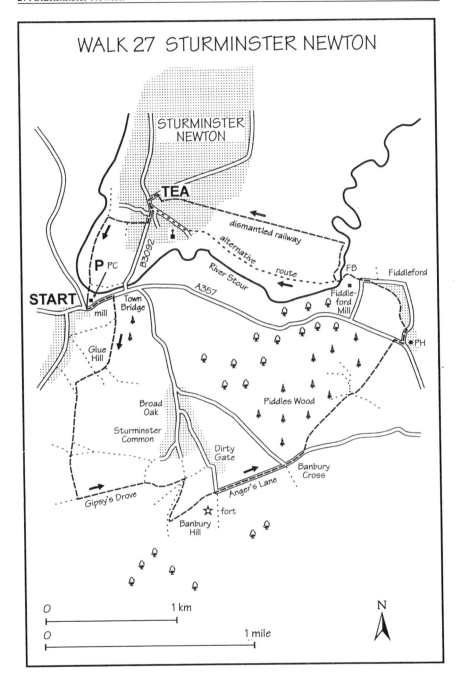

WALK 27 STURMINSTER NEWTON

cross. Turn right at Rickells Lane, pass the recreation ground and playing fields, heading for 'R. Stour'. Turn left at a 'Sturminster Mill ½' signpost and go through a waymarked gate to take the obvious path heading for the mill, in view ahead. Go through a kissing gate and cross the bridge to return to the mill and the car park above.

```
┌─────────────────────────────────────────────────────────┐
│                                                         │
│              28. Sherborne                              │
│                                                         │
└─────────────────────────────────────────────────────────┘
```

Length	6¾ miles (a shorter version is set out below)
Summary	A half day circuit based on the lovely old town of Sherborne. Generally level, with minimal ascents. With the exception of some cattle-churned mud, first rate underfoot. Mostly open country but with some woodland. Largely within Sherborne Park, the extensive estate of Sherborne Castle. Just over one mile along a quiet minor road. and one roadside mile back into town.
Car Parking	Large pay and display car park, Culverhayes, at south end of Sherborne. Public conveniences. Grid reference 641164.
Maps	Ordnance Survey Explorer no. 129, Yeovil and Sherborne, 1:25,000 or Landranger no. 183, Yeovil and Frome, 1:50,000.

Tea Shop

On market days The Three Wishes Café is hidden from view by stalls, so look carefully. This is a very typical small-town long-established café. The speciality is the "Sherbourne Stodger" – a doughy spiced cake with dried fruit – very good toasted. It is made from a very old local recipe and buns were sold at seven for 6d in 1920. Also enjoyed for tea were the ginger and honey scones served with butter and apricot jam. Dorset apple cake was served warm and with cream. If a high tea tempts the appetite following quite a long walk, ham and eggs are served with chipped potatoes, tuna and pasta bake is offered and local mackerel is cooked with lime and on-ion; these are just some of the cooked meals available. Good selection of tea – the usual blend is "Ashby's Builders" – in fact locals reputedly just ask for a pot of Builders!
Open: Mon – Sat, 9am – 6pm and Sun 11am – 4.30pm in main sea-son. Slightly shorter hours during other months and closed on Sun-days. Tel. 01935 817777.

About the Area

By north Dorset standards Sherborne is a sizeable town, a centre for

numerous villages in Blackmore Vale, well equipped with shops
and other useful features, including a town museum and a working
railway station on the line from London Waterloo to Exeter.

As would be expected it is also a historic town. The Saxon bishop,
Aldhelm, founded Sherborne Abbey early in the 8th century, with
the first school following later in the same century. The school was
spared when, at the Dissolution, the Abbey was largely destroyed.
Some former monastic buildings now form part of the school; the
14th century conduit where the monks washed also remains, at the
foot of the main street. Aldhelm's abbey church became a cathedral
until 1075, when the seat of the bishop was moved to Old Sarum.
Despite losing its bishop, the abbey church was renovated and extended in the 12th and 15th centuries. A little Saxon and much more
Norman work can still be seen in this impressive building, now
known simply as Sherborne Abbey, one of the great religious houses
of the south-west.

Also ancient is the first Sherborne Castle, a gaunt ruin of a fortress
built more than 900 years ago by Bishop Roger. Given to Sir Walter
Raleigh by Queen Elizabeth I, in 1617 the castle and estate passed to
the Digby family. Raleigh had already commenced the construction
of a new castle/stately home in 1594; in due course this became the
home of the Digby family and the old castle was allowed to fall into
ruin. The 'new' castle is still the Digby family home and, with its
grounds, laid out by Capability Brown, is open to the public from
Easter Saturday to the end of September from 1.30pm to 5.30pm on
Thursday, Saturday, Sunday and Bank Holiday Mondays. The
grounds are open one hour earlier each day. Inside, the house has
fine paintings, books, porcelain, family treasures and the usual facilities.

The Walk

Leave the car park at the lower entrance, turning right along
Ludbourne Road. At the next junction, by the Pageant Inn, turn left,
cross the River Yeo and the railway line to rise up Gas House Hill to a
'T' junction. Cross the road to a kissing gate with a yellow arrow
waymark.

Go to the left along a grass path rising gently across the hillside to a
tall kissing gate at the top; the view now includes both castles and
the end of Sherborne Lake. The path continues as a generous re-

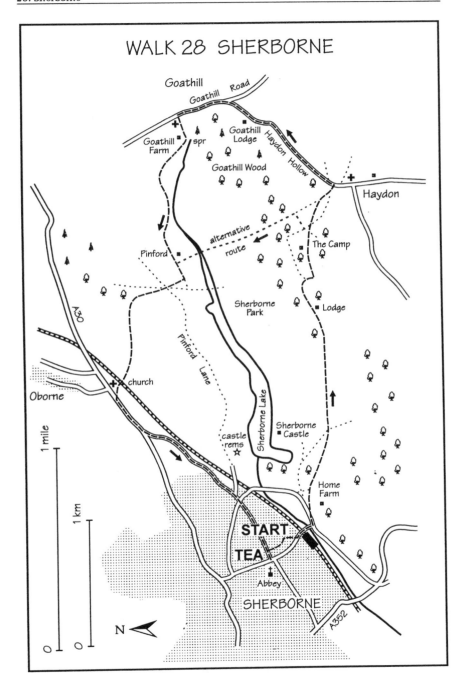

WALK 28 SHERBORNE

served strip between ploughed fields. After another old kissing gate, the broad, stony, track rises towards an area of scattered trees. Pass an unoccupied thatched lodge and climb the steepest rise so far, fortunately quite short.

Continue to another kissing gate and woodland, noting a castle keep-like structure to the right. At the far edge of a narrow wood bear left through 'The Camp' to reach an area of corrugated industrial buildings. Keep to the right of the buildings to regain open country along the surfaced access roadway.

For a shorter walk the Ordnance Survey shows a public footpath raking back sharply to the left at about 20 degrees west of north, with a start almost opposite a single storey brick agricultural building. On the ground it is not easy to locate this path and it does seem to be more straightforward to make a left turn at the edge of 'The Camp' woodland, followed by a right turn in less than 100m. In either case, a fairly straight route leads to the farm at Pinford in just under one mile, where the full circuit is rejoined.

For the full circuit follow the roadway through a substantial property, then turn sharp left along a minor public road, quietly descending to Haydon Hollow before rising past Goathill Lodge and a road junction to reach Goathill. The woods hereabouts are carpeted with bluebells in Spring, with campion in the roadside banks. Milborne Port is the village with prominent church tower in view ahead.

At Goathill turn left through a waymarked gate to pass between the farm and the tiny church. Go straight on through another gate. At a junction of farm tracks there is another waymark. Go straight on; the right of way stays close to the stream on the left but, despite cattle churning, the better route seems to be to stay close to the hedge on the right. At a gate/stile go through/over and continue to bend left towards Pinford (farm)

Go through a gate with a right turn waymark and follow the right-hand edge of the field to another churned area to the right of the main part of the farm, fortunately soon reaching a concrete driveway to leave the farm. At a junction turn right to head for a gap in a wall, flanked by a handsome pair of gate pillars. Fifteen metres after the pillars turn left at a waymark to descend a broad track. In a further 40m turn right at a waymarked post to follow a narrow but clear path through the woodland.

Go over a waymarked stile at the edge of the wood to cross a meadow on a faint path, to a gate in the far boundary. Bear a little to the left across the next field, aiming for two stiles and a plank bridge over a tiny stream. Bear a little to the right to head for an obvious bridge under the railway line.

In a few metres after the bridge there is a waymarked post and a very old slab stile beside an old wall, followed by a track direct to the main A30 road. To the left is the redundant church of St Catherine. Turn left along the roadside footpath for about 500m then turn left by the Sherborne boundary at a 'town centre' signpost. At this junction a few metres of road can be avoided by using a short length of footpath on the left.

The ruins of the old castle are in sight as the road leads back into town. Go straight on at a road junction, along Long Street, bounded by a most attractive array

Redundant church of St Catherine Oborne

of houses, mainly in stone and of all shapes and sizes and varied roof lines, heading for the Abbey. As Long Street reaches the main shopping street, turn right for a short distance to the tea shop.

From the tea shop turn right to return to the car park, either by Long Street or by continuing south to turn left into Ludbourne Road. In the latter case a visit to the Abbey requires a short deviation to the right at the first road junction.

Tea Shop Walks - Spreading everywhere!

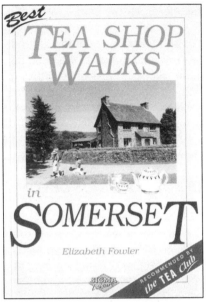

The Sigma Leisure Tea Shop Walks series already includes:

Cheshire

The Chilterns

The Cotswolds

The Lake District, Volume 1

The Lake District, Volume 2

Lancashire

Leicestershire & Rutland

North Devon

The Peak District

Shropshire

Snowdonia

Somerset

South Devon

Staffordshire

Surrey & Sussex

Warwickshire

The Yorkshire Dales

Each book costs £6.95 and contains an average of 25 excellent walks: far better value than any other competitor!

WALKS IN MYSTERIOUS SOMERSET

27 walks, of an average length of six miles, lead you into the mystical countryside of Somerset and a world of discovery. Discover the giant figures of the Glastonbury Zodiac, hear the legends of King Arthur, and quiver at the tales of the Witch of Wookey Hole whilst walking in 'enchanting' countryside! These routes are suitable for all abilities and are easily accessible by public transport.
£6.95

WALKS IN MYSTERIOUS DEVON

Is there really a Beast of Exmoor? Do Devonshire pixies exist? Might the mysterious standing stones scattered across the landscape of Devon guide you to buried treasure? Here, on almost 30 splendid walks, you can discover the legends and folklore of Exmoor, Dartmoor and beyond in the company of Trevor Beer, a local naturalist and outdoor writer.
£6.95

Companion guides are published by Sigma for Walks in Mysterious Wiltshire, Hampshire, and several other spooky locations in the UK!

In case of difficulty, or for a free catalogue, please contact:
SIGMA LEISURE, 1 SOUTH OAK LANE, WILMSLOW, CHESHIRE SK9 6AR.
Phone: 01625-531035
Fax: 01625-536800.
E-mail: sigma.press@zetnet.co.uk .
Web site: http//www.sigmapress.co.uk

VISA and MASTERCARD orders welcome.